Catholicism Under The Microscope

by
Greg Litmer

Truth
Publications

Taking His hand,
Helping each other home.
TM

ISBN 10: 1-58427-266-X

ISBN 13: 978-158427-266-3

First Printing: 2009

Truth Publications, Inc.
CEI Bookstore
220 S. Marion St., Athens, AL 35611
855-492-6657
sales@truthpublications.com
www.truthbooks.com

Table of Contents

Dedication

I dedicate this work to my mother and father. They both taught and allowed me to think for myself. Both of them left this world as devout Roman Catholics. I love them more than I could ever say. This book is further dedicated to those in my family and countless friends who remain within the confines of Roman Catholicism. To you I say, as Paul wrote to the Galatians, "Have I therefore become your enemy by telling you the truth?" (Gal. 4:16).

Why I Wrote This Book

As a small child growing up Roman Catholic, I spent every weekday morning of the school year attending eight o'clock mass at Saint John's the Evangelist, a parish in Cincinnati, Ohio. The nuns, who were our teachers, would lead each class into the church building to sit in our assigned seats and watch the sacrament of the Holy Eucharist take place. The language of the mass was Latin, which none of us understood. We did not understand the significance of each part of the mass, or the symbolism involved, but we knew by heart our assigned responses and would join in whole-heartedly at the appropriate times. If the day happened to be the first Friday of the month, we would receive a special treat. All of us would receive Communion on that day, and since it was necessary to fast from midnight until Communion had been received, the cafeteria would be opened after mass for breakfast. We did not fully understand the fast; we simply knew that not to do so was a sin.

Of course, Sunday was a particularly special day, for on that day my entire family would attend eleven o'clock mass to fulfill the requirement of worshipping God on Sunday. It was exciting to see the large numbers of my fellow Catholics gathered together doing the things I had been taught that all Christians had done since the time of Christ. We were a peculiar people, different from all the others, and we were the only ones destined to go to heaven. I knew this to be true because that was what I was taught. As a youngster I studied from *The Baltimore Catechism,* and the Catechism said:

> All are obliged to belong to the Catholic Church in order to be saved. The principle, "It makes no difference what religion a person practices so long as he leads a good life," is deceptive because it attaches the same importance to the teaching and practice of a false religion as it does to the teaching and practice of the one, true religion revealed by Christ and taught by His Church. No one

can be saved without sanctifying grace, and the Catholic Church alone is the divinely established means by which grace is brought to the world and the full fruits of Our Lord's Redemption are applied to men. When we say, "Outside the Church there is no salvation," we mean that those who through their own grave fault do not know that the Catholic Church is the true Church, or, knowing it, refuse to join it, cannot be saved (129,130).

What a joy it was to be with my fellow Catholics and to know without a doubt that we were following the teaching of Jesus more closely than any others. We were the only ones who did not eat meat on Friday, for to do so was a sin. We were the ones who had an unmarried clergy, just like Jesus was unmarried. We were the ones who were led by the infallible Pope, the Vicar of Christ and successor to Saint Peter. I was taught, as were all Catholics, that these things we did and believed had always been done and believed by all Christians from the time that Jesus established the Church until now. There was comfort in that knowledge. Even though we did not understand many of the things the Church required, we were secure in our belief that this was the way it had always been, and that this was the way that it would always be. The Roman Catholic Church was truth, and truth did not change. Catholics such as myself found solace and comfort in that belief.

Then came the years of 1962-1965 and an event that radically changed the face of Roman Catholicism as it existed at the time. On October 11, 1962, 2,540 bishops and others of the Roman Catholic Church gathered in Rome for the opening solemn session of Vatican II. By the time of the final solemn session, held December 8, 1965, the comfort and solace that so many Roman Catholics had found in their Church had been changed. It was no longer the same. For many Roman Catholics there was confusion; for many elderly Roman Catholics there was a feeling of betrayal – how could things that they had been taught and practiced for so many years no longer be either true or required? For many younger Catholics, such as myself, we went along with the direction the Church was taking until the changes simply became too much to embrace. The Roman Catholic Church, the Church of our Fathers (or so I thought) had radically changed and I ceased to be a practicing Catholic.

I am often asked why I left the Catholic Church. That is a good question. After leaving the Church of my youth, my study of it actually deepened. Much of what I found you will find in this book.

Roman Catholic Mariology

In the book, *What the Church Teaches*, Father J.D. Conway states, "Nothing is more distinctly Catholic than devotion to the Blessed Virgin Mary." Those familiar with the outpouring of devotion toward Mary, the mother of Jesus, and the numerous doctrines concerning her in Roman Catholicism recognize the truthfulness of Conway's statement.

In *The Catechism of the Catholic Church* (251, #963), we find, "The Virgin Mary is acknowledged and honored as being truly the Mother of God and of the redeemer. She is clearly the mother of the members of Christ, since she has by her charity joined in bringing about the birth of believers in the Church, who are members of its head. Mary, Mother of Christ, Mother of the Church."

Well do I remember my days as a student at St. John the Evangelist in Cincinnati, Ohio. Each May, one eighth-grade girl would be chosen from her class to receive the honor of placing a crown upon a statue of Mary that stood in the churchyard. The entire school took part in the procession leading up to the climax—her crowning. It was a marvelously inspiring ceremony, and as a child it never occurred to me to ask where it came from.

Here we are going to address certain aspects of the Roman Catholic system of Mariology. We are going to ask what it is, where it came from, whether or not God authorized such devotion to Mary, and whether or not God actually taught in His revealed Word the various doctrines concerning Mary found in Catholicism.

What about Mary in the Scriptures? She appears in the following New Testament passages. Obviously, Mary is found in the narratives concerning the events surrounding the birth of our Lord in Matthew 1 and 2 and Luke 1 and 2. We can read of Mary at "…the wedding feast in Cana" (John 2:1-11). We also read of her in the events described in Matthew 12:46 and Mark 3:21-35. Again we find Mary at the cross of Jesus (John 19:25-27). And finally we read of Mary in the upper room in Jerusalem (Acts 1:14), this being the last time that she is mentioned in Scripture. There she is said to be joined with the disciples and other women in prayer and supplication along with the brethren of Jesus. In the twenty-two books of the New Testament that follow the Acts of the Apostles, Mary is not mentioned. John, who was entrusted with her care by Jesus, does not mention her in any of his three epistles or in the book of Revelation. We can also say that in a prophetic sense Mary is spoken of in the Old Testament as "…the seed of woman" (Gen. 3:15) and in the prophecy of the virgin birth (Isa. 7:14). No matter where we look in the pages of God's Word, we do not find Mary to be the object of special veneration or extraordinary honor. Certainly at no time can we read of a prayer being offered to her or through her.

The International Standard Bible Encyclopedia (III: 2005) gives this summation of what we can learn about Mary from the biblical accounts concerning her:

> The sum of the matter concerning Mary seems to be this: The mother of Jesus was a typical Jewish believer of the best sort. She was deeply meditative, but by no means a daring or original thinker. Her inherited Messianic beliefs did not and perhaps could not prepare her for the method of Jesus which involved so much that was new and unexpected. But her heart was true, and from the beginning to the day of Pentecost, she pondered in her heart the meaning of her many puzzling experiences until the light came. The story of her life and of her relationship to Jesus is consistent throughout and touched with manifold unconscious traits of truth. Such a narrative could not have been feigned or fabled.

There is absolutely nothing in God's Word that even remotely resembles Roman Catholic Mariology. So where did it come from, and what does it involve?

It is safe and correct to say that the early church knew nothing of what has come to be called Mariology. Standing in sharp contrast to the biblical accounts, there appeared certain apocryphal writings in the latter part of the second century that greatly expanded upon Mary's role and did so in legendary fashion. The most prominent of these was called *The Protoevangelium of James*. In this work, all sorts of things about Mary are stated, such as the names of her parents, that she stayed for a time in the temple as a little girl, a rather imaginative story about her birth, and the belief that she remained a virgin throughout her life. Roman Catholic authorities have rejected this work as spurious, yet they have absorbed many of its legends into their system of Mariology.

Mary – "Ever Virgin"

In Isaiah 7:14 we find, "Therefore the Lord himself shall give you a sign: Behold, a virgin shall conceive, and bear a son, and shall call his name Immanuel." Here is the prophecy concerning the miraculous character of the birth of Jesus. He would be born of a virgin. The gospel accounts of the events surrounding His birth demonstrate that this came to pass. Let us read just one:

> Now the birth of Jesus Christ was on this wise: When his mother Mary was espoused to Joseph, before they came together, she was found with child of the Holy Ghost. Then Joseph her husband, being a just man, and not willing to make her a public example, was minded to put her away privily. But while he thought on these things, behold, the angel of the Lord appeared unto him in a dream, saying, Joseph, thou son of David, fear not to take unto thee Mary thy wife, for that which is conceived in her is of the Holy Ghost. And she shall bring forth a son, and thou shalt call his name Jesus: for he shall save his people from their sins. Now all this was done, that it might be fulfilled which was spoken of the Lord by the prophet, saying, Behold, a virgin shall be with child, and shall bring forth a son, and they shall call his name Immanuel, which being interpreted is, God with us. Then Joseph being raised from sleep did as the angel of the Lord had bidden him, and took unto him his wife: and knew her not till she had brought forth her first-born son: and he called his name Jesus (Matt. 1:18-25).

Jesus was born of a virgin, meaning that Mary conceived Jesus in a miraculous way, by the Holy Spirit without having "known" a man prior to the birth. That is easy enough to understand.

Jesus was born of a virgin, meaning that Mary conceived Jesus in a miraculous way, by the Holy Spirit without having "known" a man prior to the birth. That is easy enough to understand. That is what we have been told in the Scriptures, and all who respect the Word of God must believe it.

At the time of the conception of Jesus, Mary was espoused to Joseph. We could equate this with being engaged today, although an espousal was much more serious than an engagement. In his book, *Twenty-Five Questions Non-Catholics Ask*, John A. O'Brien, a professor of research at the University of Notre Dame, says, "As Mary had already dedicated herself by a vow or at least a firm resolve to a life of virginity, she asks: 'How shall this be, seeing I know not a man?'" (84). Now I ask you, is there anything in this passage that even hints that Mary had dedicated herself by a vow, or by a firm resolve, to a life of virginity? Was there anything in Matthew 1 that could lead us to this conclusion? Much to the contrary! Reading that she was espoused to Joseph hardly indicates one who intended to lead a life of perpetual virginity.

The Roman Catholic Church has a great deal to say about the virginity of Mary; indeed, a whole lot more than God ever did. Not content with what has been revealed, Roman Catholic theologians and scholars have allowed their imaginations to run wild, resulting in an elaborate doctrine that can be called, "The Perpetual Virginity of Mary." *The Catechism of the Catholic Church* (126, #499), states it this way, "The deepening of faith in the virginal motherhood led the Church to confess Mary's real and perpetual virginity even in the act of giving birth to the Son of God made man. In fact, Christ's birth did not diminish his mother's virginal integrity but sanctified it. And so the liturgy of the Church celebrates Mary as the 'Ever-virgin.'"

This belief involves three stages of Mary's virginity: her conception of Jesus without the cooperation of man, giving birth to Christ without violating her integrity, and remaining a virgin after Jesus was born. This belief did not come into being in its entirety all at once but gradually developed over a period of hundreds of years. Let's examine that development, notice exactly what these beliefs concerning Mary involve, and determine whether or not they are purely the speculation of man or if they have their basis in divine truth.

Very early in the existence of the church, Christians found it necessary to defend the virgin birth of our Lord because of its denial by various groups. They denied the divinity of Jesus as born from Mary and taught that the child conceived in Mary's womb was solely man and not divine until after His birth. In the second century, the Gnostics, under Cerinthus, voiced opposition to the revealed truth that Jesus was born of a virgin. Then in the third century, opposition came from a group led by Celsus. In response to these denials the early Christians stood firmly upon the Word of God. Such men as Ignatius of Antioch and Justin Martyr uniformly defended the accounts of the virgin birth as given by Matthew and Luke in their gospels. What they defended was what had been revealed—Jesus had miraculously been conceived in the womb of Mary by the Holy Spirit. She was a virgin when this occurred and remained a virgin until the birth of our Lord. If men had been content with what God had revealed there would be no such thing today as the Catholic doctrine concerning the virginity of Mary. But they were not.

The Council of Ephesus declared Mary the "mother of God" in A.D. 431. From this decree the theologians engaged in all sorts of speculation. Some began to teach that not only did Mary conceive without carnal intercourse, but also that her physical virginity was not violated in giving birth to Christ. As early as A.D. 390 we can find the synod at Milan condemning the proposition that "a virgin conceived, but a virgin did not bring forth." Without going into physiological detail, this proposition was not teaching that after the conception, but prior to the birth, Mary had relations with Joseph. Rather it was teaching that, in the natural course of things, during the birth the passage was opened. Uninspired men denied that that was true.

In *The Book of Catholic Quotations*, Augustine, the noted fifth century Catholic scholar, wrote, "For as a virgin she conceived, as a virgin she gave birth, a virgin she remained." He also wrote, "For neither do we know the countenance of the Virgin Mary, from whom, untouched by a husband, nor tainted in the birth itself, He was wonderfully born" (51).

Also from *The Book of Catholic Quotations,* in his *Commentary on the Apostles' Creed* from the fifth century, Rufinus wrote, "The gate which was shut (Ezech. 44,2) was her virginity. Through it the Lord God of Israel entered; through it He advanced into this world from the Virgin's womb. And, because her virginity was preserved intact, the Virgin's gate has remained shut forever" (9).

Collier's Encyclopedia, (XV, #472), tells us, "Ancient writers such as Ambrose, Augustine, and Jerome employ various analogies—the emergence of Christ from the sealed tomb, the penetration of light through glass, or human thought leaving the mind" to explain how Jesus could have been born and yet Mary remain intact.

Having taken this step in their thinking, uninspired men took yet another. Since Mary had conceived as a virgin, and since she remained "intact" in the birth of Christ, they reasoned that she surely must have remained a virgin for the rest of her life, never engaging in normal marital relations with her husband, Joseph. *Collier's Encyclopedia* (XV: 472) gives these words from the fourth-century writer, Basil: "The friends of Christ do not tolerate hearing that the Mother of God ever ceased to be a virgin." By the Fifth General Council of Constantinople in A.D. 553, Mary had received the title, "Perpetual Virgin." Today the *New Baltimore Catechism* says, "Mary, the Mother of God, remained a virgin not only in the conception of Christ but also in His birth and during the rest of her life" (3, #49).

Such passages as, "Is not this the carpenter's son? Is not his mother called Mary? And his brethren, James, and Joses, and Simon and Judas? And his sisters, are they not all with us? Whence then hath this man all these things?" (Matt. 13:55-56) are explained away by Roman Catholic authorities in the following manner, taken from *The Catechism of the Catholic Church* (126, #500):

> Against this doctrine the objection is sometimes raised that the Bible mentions brothers and sisters of Jesus. The Church has always understood these passages as not referring to other children of the Virgin Mary. In fact James and Joseph, 'brothers of Jesus,' are the sons of another Mary, a disciple of Christ, whom St. Matthew significantly calls 'the other Mary.' They are close relations of Jesus, according to an Old Testament expression.

That sounds very good except for the fact that the word used for "brethren" (*adelphos*) in Matthew 13:55 means "male children of the same mother," just as it does in 1 Corinthians 9:5 and Galatians 1:19 (*Vine's Expository Dictionary of New Testament Words*, 154). If Matthew had wanted to say that these individuals were our Lord's cousins, he could have said so by using the word *sungenis*. These men—James, Joses, Simon, and Judas—were His actual brothers; therefore, Mary was not a perpetual virgin.

There is another very serious issue raised by the doctrine of "the perpetual virginity of Mary." The Bible teaches that the marriage bed is undefiled (Heb. 13:4) and that a husband and wife have the God-given responsibility to tend to the sexual needs of each other (1 Cor. 7). If Mary remained a virgin throughout her life, then she and Joseph were husband and wife in appearance only and did not fulfill their obligations to one another. That is a clear violation of God's decrees concerning this holiest of human relationships.

We can get an idea of the type of thinking that gave rise to this doctrine in *Twenty-Five Questions Non-Catholics Ask* from a fourth century letter of Siricius, who wrote:

> We surely cannot deny that you were right in correcting the doctrine about children of Mary, and Your Holiness was right in rejecting the idea that any other offspring should come from the same virginal womb from which Christ was born according to the flesh. For the Lord Jesus would not have chosen to be born of a virgin if he had judged that she would be so incontinent as to taint the birthplace of the body of the Lord, the home of the eternal king, with the seed of human intercourse (87).

Matthew 1:25 states, "And knew her not till she had brought forth her first-born son: and he called his name Jesus." A simple, unprejudiced reading of that passage shows that Mary and Joseph did not engage in sexual relationships until after Jesus was born. According to O'Brien, the key to understanding that passage rests with the two words "till" and "first-born." He says that the word "till" "may indicate a point of time up to which a state, an action or inaction continues, without implying any change thereafter." As a reference, he cites Isaiah 46:4. He renders the first part of that verse, "I am—till you grow old." He says, "Here the state of God's being continues unchanged—the same afterward as before. So too did the state of Mary's virginity remain unchanged." A simple rule of understanding the Bible says that the meaning must make sense in context. I agree with what he says about Isaiah 46:4. That's exactly what was being said—it makes sense and fits the context. But to use that same reasoning in Matthew 1:25 does not make sense. The context clearly shows that after the birth of Jesus, Mary and Joseph lived in a normal husband and wife relationship.

Truly there would have been absolutely nothing incontinent about Mary fulfilling her obligation as a wife. Indeed, this doctrine forces one to believe that she was negligent in her duties to her husband. This doctrine is just one example of what happens when men allow their imaginations to run free.

The Bodily Assumption of Mary into Heaven
Pope Pius XII only officially declared this doctrine in the Catholic system of Mariology on November 1, 1950. The following is found in the *Book of Catholic Quotations*:

> By the authority of our Lord Jesus Christ, of the blessed apostles Peter and Paul, and by our own authority, we pronounce, declare and define it to be a

divinely revealed dogma: that the immaculate Mother of God, the ever Virgin Mary, having completed the course of her earthly life, was assumed body and soul into heavenly glory (41).

The *Catechism of the Catholic Church* (252, #966) says:

> Finally the Immaculate Virgin, preserved free from all stain of original sin, when the course of her earthly life was finished, was taken up body and soul into heavenly glory, and exalted by the Lord as Queen over all things, so that she might be the more fully conformed to her Son, the Lord of lords and conqueror of sin and death.

Thus, with the words of the original declaration and the statement from the 1994 edition of the *Catechism*, we see the doctrine of the bodily assumption of Mary into heaven formally defined and stated as an article of faith in the Roman Catholic Church. How this idea reached the level of an "article of faith" is a tale of pure speculation, human reasoning, fanciful flights of imagination, and complete disregard for scriptural or historical evidence.

The following is a quote from an authorized Catholic source, *The Question Box*, written by Bertrand L. Conway, bearing the Imprimatur of Patrick Cardinal Hayes. This book was written in 1929, before the Assumption was declared to be an article of faith, and gives some interesting insights into the doctrine:

> Question: Is there any biblical or historical proof of the ascension of the Virgin Mary into heaven? Is the Assumption a dogma of the faith?
>
> Answer: The dogma of the Assumption means the Blessed Virgin's entrance into heaven, body and soul by the power of God. The active term Ascension is used only of Jesus Christ's entrance into heaven by His own divine power. The doctrine has never been defined by the Church, although its wide acceptance since the sixth century renders it a certain doctrine, that cannot be denied by Catholics without rashness.
>
> It cannot be proved from the Bible, or from contemporary historical witnesses, but it rests on such solid theological principles, that many Bishops have written the Apostolic See, requesting its definition as a dogma of faith.
>
> Some may think it strange that the Fathers of the first five centuries do not mention it. But as St. Augustine says: 'There are many things that the universal Church maintains and that we reasonably believe were preached by the Apostles, although they never have been put in writing' (De Bapt., v. 23). We can readily conjecture reasons for their silence. Perhaps they feared that certain heretics, like the Valentinians, might cite this doctrine in proof of their errors concerning

the Body of Christ. Perhaps again they wished to keep the cultus of the Blessed Virgin in the background on account of the prevalent idolatry. Moreover, when bitter controversy was being waged on such important dogmas as the Trinity and the Incarnation, less important doctrines might well be ignored.

It certainly seems most fitting that the body of the Immaculate Mother of God should not taste corruption, and that it should share in the triumph of her Son, the Risen Christ. Kellner tells us that the feast of the Assumption in the East is older than the sixth century, for it was celebrated by the heretical sects that separated from Rome in the fifth century, viz., the Monophysites, the Nestorians, the Armenians, and the Ethiopians. The most ancient writer to speak of it in the West is St. Gregory of Tours (539) who writes, "The Lord had the most holy body of the Virgin taken into heaven, where, reunited to her soul, it now enjoys with the elect, happiness without end" (361-362).

Just from these few sentences from an authorized Catholic source we find it admitted that there is no scriptural evidence to support the doctrine of the Assumption of Mary, nor is there any contemporary historical evidence to substantiate it. We also find it admitted that for the first five centuries, the early church was completely silent on the subject. How do they deal with this lack of evidence? Well, *The Manual of Catholic Theology* says, "Mary's corporeal assumption into heaven is so thoroughly implied in the notion of her personality as given by Bible and dogma, that the church can dispense with strict historical evidence of the fact." I suppose when we can dispense with the need for evidence, we can believe just about anything.

We also saw in the statements from *The Question Box* that the earliest western writer to speak of the assumption of Mary was Gregory of Tours. Nothing is said in *The Question Box* of the nature of what Gregory wrote, but *In Glorium Martyrum*, his work that was referred to, we see little more than a fairy tale. Gregory tells of Mary dying with the apostles gathered around her bed. Into this scene Jesus appears with His angels and commits the soul of Mary to Gabriel and her body is carried away in a cloud. There is no more evidence for the truth of this legend than there is for the ghost stories Boy Scouts tell around the campfire. Yet this legend has grown into an official doctrine of the Roman Catholic Church.

The statement in *The Question Box* told us that the doctrine rested upon solid theological principles. What are those principles? A little further in *The Question Box* we find, "It certainly seems most fitting that the body of the Immaculate Mother of God should not taste corruption" (361). Once more from the *Book of Catholic Quotations* we quote from the eighth century writer, John of Damascus:

> It was fitting that she who had kept her virginity intact in childbirth, should keep her own body free from all corruption even after death. It was fitting that she, who had carried the Creator as a Child at her breast, should dwell in the divine tabernacles. It was fitting that the spouse, whom the Father had taken to Himself, should live in the divine mansion. It was fitting that she, who had seen her son upon the Cross and who had thereby received into her heart the sword of sorrow which she had escaped in the act of giving birth to Him, should look upon Him as He sits at the right hand of the Father. It was fitting that God's Mother should possess what belongs to her Son, and that she should be honored by every creature as the Mother and as the Handmaid of God (39).

Even *Collier's Encyclopedia* (XV: 473) says, "In the absence of a dogmatic pronouncement, modern theologians generally believe that Mary died. Though they admit she was not bound by the law of mortality, because of her exemption from sin, they believe it was fitting that Mary's body should resemble that of her Son, who allowed Himself to die for the salvation of men."

I think we can see the "solid theological principles" upon which this doctrine rests can be summed up with the words, "It certainly seems fitting." In other words, "It seems like it ought to be true, therefore it is." I wonder if any Roman Catholic theologian would like to be tried for a crime on the basis of "It certainly seems fitting that he did it" or if he would be willing to "dispense with strict historical evidence of the fact."

Four years before defining the Assumption of Mary as an article of faith, Pius XII asked all of the bishops in communion with Rome whether or not they believed it, and if so, whether or not a solemn declaration was in order. Practically the whole episcopate answered "yes" to both questions, so Pius XII decided to make it official. The solid theological principles utilized were, "It certainly seems fitting" and "We believe it, therefore it is true." It has been readily admitted that there is no scriptural or historical evidence to sustain this doctrine.

They Say They Don't Worship Mary, But...

I can envision a Roman Catholic priest reading the title of this section and thinking, "There goes another one, claiming that we worship Mary, and that is not true!" In many authorized Roman Catholic books it is denied that the Roman Church teaches that Mary is to be worshipped. The position is taken that Mary is viewed as a human being, a highly exalted human being, but only a human being and in no way equal with God. Yet in the face of such denials, it is obvious that a great deal of emphasis is placed upon Mary and devotion to her.

In the book, *What the Church Teaches* by Conway, which bears the Nihil Obstat and the Imprimatur (official declarations that a book or pamphlet is free of doctrinal or moral error), this statement is made:

> God's Mother is worthy of honor. He honored her Himself in choosing her from among all his creatures. We never forget the basic truth of our religion: there is only one God, *and He alone is to be worshipped.* But that does not mean that we are forbidden to pay reasonable, sensible honor to creatures. God explicitly commands you to honor your own father and mother. Is it then wrong to honor God's Mother?

> From the beginning, the Church has given to Mary the highest form of honor that can be properly given to any creature. *She is human, just as we are. We must never adore her; that is for God alone. But otherwise we cannot honor her to excess, because it is not possible to overestimate the privileges God gave her in making her His own Mother.*

> Most of the opposition to Catholic devotion to Mary results from a misunderstanding of the nature of that devotion. *We do not try to deify Mary nor make her equal to God in any respect.*

Despite statements such as this, it is obvious that within the Roman Catholic Church a great deal of emphasis is placed upon Mary. There are Holy Days of Obligation devoted to Mary, there are prayers whose subject is Mary, there are shrines devoted to Mary that are visited by thousands of pilgrims a year, there are doctrines, as we have seen, that separate Mary from all others. The Catholic Church teaches that Mary was born without sin, while all others were born in sin. It teaches that Mary lived her life free from sin. It teaches that she is the Co-Mediatrix with Christ. It calls her Virgin of Virgins, Mother of God, Queen of Sorrows, Refuge of Sinners, Virgin Most Merciful, and on and on. It certainly raises the question that, if such is not worship, what is it?

Roman Catholic theologians, recognizing that there is no scriptural authorization for their attitude toward Mary, have arrived at the following formula, presented in the 1917 *Code of Canon Law*, Canon 1255 (20th century), to distinguish between the worship given to God and what they give to Mary. The canon reads:

The worship due to the most holy Trinity, to each of the divine Persons, to our Lord Jesus Christ, even under the sacramental species, is called *cultus latriae* (highest kind of worship, adoration); that which is due to the blessed Virgin Mary is called *cultus hyperduliae* (special veneration or worship); that which is due to the others who reign with Christ in heaven is called *cultus duliae* (veneration or worship). To sacred relics and images there is also due a veneration and worship which is relative to the persons to whom the relics and images refer.

To put it simply, the Roman Catholic Church divides worship into three kinds: *latria*, the highest form of worship and given to the Godhead only; *dulia*, which is something of a secondary form of veneration that is given to saints and angels; *hyperdulia*, which is a higher form of veneration, called in the *Canon Law* a special veneration or worship. Even though such a formula is totally without scriptural precedent, it may sound plausible to the uninformed hearer. In actual practice, though, this theological formula is useless. Most Roman Catholics do not, or cannot, make the distinctions. In truth, most do not know they exist.

For example, in twelve years of parochial school education I did not once hear of *latria*, *dulia*, and *hyperdulia*. Even if I had, how could a second-grade child make such a distinction when he takes part in the May Festival Crowning of the statue of Mary, with prayers and songs being offered unto her? Each classroom had a crucifix, but each classroom had a statue of Mary as well. We were told again and again of Fatima and Lourdes, and the wondrous things that Mary was supposed to have done there. We were taught to go to Mary in prayer; indeed, the Rosary contains fifty Hail Mary's.

The true attitude that the Roman Catholic laity is taught to possess toward Mary is expressed in some of the prayers they are taught to say to her by rote. Consider the words of the Hail Mary:

Hail Mary, full of grace! The Lord is with thee; blessed art thou among women, and blessed is the fruit of thy womb, Jesus. Holy Mary, Mother of God, pray for us sinners, now and at the hour of our death. Amen.

Another prayer we were taught went like this:

Remember, O most loving Virgin Mary, that never was it known that any one who fled to thy protection, implored thy help, and sought thy intercession, was left forsaken. Filled, therefore, with confidence in thy goodness, I fly to thee, O Mother, Virgin of virgins; to thee I come, before thee I stand, sinful and sorrowful. Despise not my words, O Mother of the Word, but graciously hear and grant my prayer.

And here are the words to the prayer, Hail, Holy Queen:

> Hail, Holy queen, Mother of mercy, hail, our life, our sweetness, and our hopes! To thee do we cry, poor banished children of Eve! To thee do we send up our sighs, mourning and weeping in this vale of tears! Turn them, most gracious advocate, thine eyes of mercy towards us; and after this, our exile, show unto us the blessed fruit of thy womb, Jesus! O clement, O loving, O sweet virgin Mary!

The same things that a Catholic requests of God the Father and our Lord Jesus in Roman Catholic prayers are the same things requested of Mary. While the formula of *latria, dulia,* and *hyperdulia* does permit the Roman Catholic Church to *officially* deny worshipping Mary, its actual practice shows otherwise. God is to be the object of our honor and reverence, and we must be careful not to give honor due to Him and His Son to anyone else. The first-century church did not afford Mary any special position, and it certainly gave her no special veneration or worship. *Hyperdulia,* as well as the formula of which it is a part, is a theological attempt to justify a system of belief that promotes the worship of Mary.

I have a small book entitled, *True Devotion to the Blessed Virgin Mary,* by St. Louis Mary De Montford. It bears the Nihil Obstat of John M.A. Fearns, and the Imprimatur of Francis Cardinal Spellman. On the fourth page of this book we find the following endorsements from various popes:

> From Pius XII we find, "The force and unction of the word of Mary's servant (Blessed De Montford) have not only touched, but captivated and converted many souls."

> From Pius XI we have, "I have practiced this devotion every day since my youth."

> Benedict XV wrote, "A book of high authority and unction."

We also read on this page that "Pius XI declared that Blessed De Montford's devotion to Mary was the best and most acceptable form of devotion to our Lady." It is very safe to say, based on the authority of the popes mentioned and the Nihil Obstat and Imprimatur, that *True Devotion to the Blessed Virgin Mary* sets forth the position espoused by Roman Catholic authorities concerning Mary. If that is not true, then the infallible popes quoted were wrong.

I am going to present several statements from *True Devotion to the Blessed Virgin Mary.* We need only to read them to determine that Conway's statement, "We do not try to deify Mary nor make her equal to God in any respect" is simply not true. The following quotes are all taken from *True Devotion to the Blessed Virgin Mary*:

> Inasmuch as grace perfects nature, and glory perfects grace, it is certain that our Lord is still, in heaven, as much the Son of Mary as He was on earth; and that, consequently, He has retained the obedience and submission of the most perfect Child toward the best of all mothers (17).

> When we read then in the writing of Sts. Bernard, Bernadine, Bonaventure, and others, that in heaven and on earth everything, even God Himself, is subject to the Blessed Virgin, they mean that the authority which God has been well pleased to give her is so great that it seems as if she had the same power as God; and that her prayers and petitions are so powerful with God that they always pass for commandments with His Majesty, Who never resists the prayer of His dear Mother, because she is always humble and conformed to His will (17-18).

> In the heavens, Mary commands the angels and the blessed. As a recompense for her profound humility, God has empowered her and commissioned her to fill with saints the empty thrones from which the apostate angels fell by pride. The will of the Most High, Who exalts the humble, is that heaven, earth and hell bend, with good will or bad will, to the commandments of the humble Mary, whom He has made sovereign of heaven and earth, general of His armies, treasurer of His treasuries, dispenser of His graces, worker of His greatest marvels, restorer of the human race, mediatrix of men, the exterminator of the enemies of God, and the faithful companion of His grandeurs and triumphs (18-19).

> The learned and pious Jesuit, Suarez, the erudite and devout Justus Lipsius, doctor of Louvain, and many others have proved invincibly, from the sentiments of the Fathers (among others, St. Augustine, St. Ephrem, deacon of Edessa, St. Cyril of Jerusalem, St. Germanus of Constantinople, St. John Damascene, St. Anslem, St. Bernard, St. Bernadine, St. Thomas, and St. Bonaventure), that devotion to our Blessed Lady is necessary to salvation (25-26).

It was through Mary that the salvation of the world was begun, and it is through Mary that it must be consummated. Mary hardly appeared at all in the first coming of Jesus Christ, in order that men, as yet but little instructed and enlightened on the Person of her Son, should not remove themselves from Him in attaching themselves too strongly and too grossly to her. This would have apparently taken place if she had been known, because of the admirable charms which the Most High had bestowed upon her exterior. This is so true that St. Denis the Areopagite tells us in his writings that when he saw our

Blessed Lady, he would have taken her for a divinity, because of her secret charms and incomparable beauty (31-32).

The most terrible of all enemies which God has set up against the devil is His Holy Mother Mary. He has inspired her, even since the days of the earthy paradise, though she existed then only in His idea, with so much hatred against that cursed enemy of God, with so much ingenuity in unveiling the malice of that ancient serpent, with so much power to conquer, to overthrow and to crush that proud, impious rebel, that he fears her not only more than all angels and men, but in a sense more than God Himself (35).

What Eve has damned and lost to disobedience, Mary has saved by obedience. Eve, in obeying the serpent, has destroyed all her children together with herself, and has delivered them to him; Mary, in being perfectly faithful to God, has saved all her children and servants together with herself, and has consecrated them to His Majesty (36).

St. Anslem, St. Bernard, St. Bernadine, St. Bonaventure say: "All things, the Virgin included, are subject to the empire of God; behold, all things, and God included, are subject to the empire of the Virgin" (55).

We have three steps to mount to go to God; the first, which is nearest to us and the most suited to our capacity, is Mary; the second is Jesus Christ; and the third is God the Father. To go to Jesus, we must go to Mary; she is our mediatrix of intercessions (62-63).

It is a most glorious and praiseworthy thing, and very useful to those who have thus made themselves slaves of Jesus in Mary, that they should wear, as a sign of their loving slavery, little iron chains, blessed with the proper blessing (175).

On and on we could go, but these few quotes from an authorized Roman Catholic book suffice to show the true, official position of the Roman Catholic authorities toward Mary. Yet even as I write these words, I can almost hear the objections of various priests, demanding that we allow for the rapture of devotion in the words of the book, that we allow for the exaggeration in language of those overcome with the emotion of love for the virgin. Interestingly enough, *True Devotion to the Blessed Virgin Mary* answers those objections itself when it says:

The critical devotees are, for the most part, proud scholars, rash and self-sufficient spirits, who have at heart some devotion to the holy Virgin, but who criticize nearly all the practices of devotion which simple people pay simply and holily to the Good Mother, because these practices do not fall in with their own humor and fancy. They call in doubt all the miracles and pious stories recorded by authors worthy of faith, or drawn from the chronicles of religious orders: narratives which testify to us the mercies and the power of the most holy Virgin. They cannot see, without uneasiness, simple and humble people on their knees before an altar of an image of our Lady, sometimes at the corner of a street, in order to pray to God there; and they even accuse them of idolatry, as if they adored the wood or the stone. They say that, for their part, they are not fond of these external devotions, and that they are not so credulous as to believe so many tales and stories that are told about our Lady. When they are told how admirable the Fathers of the Church praised the Blessed Virgin, they either reply that the Fathers spoke as professional orators, with exaggeration; or they misinterpret their words. These kinds of false devotees and proud and worldly people are greatly to be feared. They do an infinite wrong to devotion to our Lady (67-68).

So, my friends, if you should be a Roman Catholic, ask your priest about the quotes presented in this book. Ask him to explain the language. If he says you must allow for exaggeration, realize that even several popes would say that he is then a man to be feared.

Mary, Mediatrix?

In the book, *What the Church Teaches*, Monsignor J.D. Conway writes:

It is the common and explicit teaching of the Church today that every grace given to men comes to them through Mary. She is the almoner for her generous Son. She hands out His treasures, as a Mother's right. Being mediatrix is simply a Mother's privilege. She was intimately associated with Her Son in everything pertaining to our Redemption and salvation while they were both on earth. Why should He change the order of things now that they are both in heaven?

Jesus Christ is the only mediator between God and Man. He brought God to us when He became man. He takes us back to God with Him through His redemptive grace. He permits us to understand something about God, first, by bringing God down to the human level, in the Incarnation; and second, by giving us a bit of divine intelligence, in Faith.

Mary, the mediatrix, brought Jesus to us, and brings us to Jesus (211-212).

Thus, in an authorized Catholic book, the teaching of Mary as "Mediatrix" is set forth. Further explanation of this peculiarly Catholic teaching is presented in *Collier's Encyclopedia* (XV: 472):

Related to Mary's position as mother of the Saviour is her dignity as intermediary between Christ and the human race. There are, however, two aspects of this mediation, which should be carefully distinguished. It is certain in Catholic theology that, since Mary gave birth to the Redeemer who is the source of all grace, she is the channel of all graces to mankind. But it is only probable, as a legitimate opinion, that, since Mary's Assumption into heaven, no grace is received by humans without her cooperation and intercession.

Such explanations of the "mediation" of Mary are utilized by Roman Catholic authorities to answer critics who charge that making Mary a "mediatrix" usurps the position of Jesus Christ. They claim to teach that Jesus is the only mediator between God and man and that Roman Catholic teaching concerning Mary does not interfere with that. What it does do is to add another step to what God has decreed. Jesus is the mediator between God and man, but to get to Jesus, one must go through Mary. Two things stand out about this doctrine. Number one is that it is a completely man-made doctrine, the result of human reasoning and imagination that began back with Mary being defined as the "Mother of God" by the Council of Ephesus in A.D. 431 and has continued to grow and be added to unto this day. The second major thing about this teaching that stands out is that, regardless of claims to the contrary, it does indeed usurp the position of Christ as the "One Mediator" between God and man and adds a step in the mediatorial process that God did not put there; namely, Mary.

Within Roman Catholicism's history, few men have promoted the growth of Mariology to the extent that Alphonse de Liguori has. Liguori was born in 1696 in Naples. He was well educated, receiving his degree at the age of sixteen, and entered into the practice of law. At the age of thirty he was ordained a priest, and at thirty-six he founded the Redemptorist religious congregations. Around the age of fifty he began to write. He was canonized in 1839 and declared a Doctor of the Church in 1871 by Pope Pius IX. In 1950 Pope Pius XII declared him to be the patron saint of all confessors and moral theologians. Liguori is an authoritative source of Roman Catholic doctrine and practice, and his recognized area of expertise was Mariology. Perhaps his best-known book is called *The Glories of Mary*, which bears the Nihil Obstat of Edward A. Cerny, S.S., S.T.D.; and the Imprimatur of Lawrence J. Shehan, D.D., Archibishop of Baltimore. We are going to notice a few statements from that book and compare them with what God's Word has to say, but before doing that I want to notice the editor's comments from the 1931 edition of *The Glories of Mary*, where he wrote:

> Everything that our saint has written is, as it were, a summary of Catholic tradition on the subject that it treats; it is, so to speak, the church herself that speaks to us by the voice of her prophets, her apostles, her pontiffs, her saints,

her fathers, her doctors of nations and ages. No other book appears to be more worthy of recommendation in this respect than *The Glories of Mary*.

It is important to realize that as we read Liguori's comments we are reading the Roman Catholic position. As we saw, it is not so much Liguori speaking, as the Roman Catholic Church herself. Let's notice whether the teaching of Mary as "Mediatrix" usurps the position of Jesus or not:

Mary is our life…Mary in obtaining this grace for sinners by her intercession, thus restores them to life (80). And she is truly a mediatress of peace between sinners and God. Sinners receive pardon by…Mary alone (82-83).

He fails and is lost who has not recourse to Mary (94).

The Way of Salvation is open to none otherwise than through Mary, our salvation is in the hands of Mary…He who is protected by Mary will be saved, he who is not will be lost (169-170).

(Mary) is also the Advocate of the whole human race…for she can do what she wills with God (193).

Mary is the Peace-maker between sinners and God (197).

How do these statements by Liguori compare with the Word of God? We can see for ourselves:

For there is one God, and one mediator between God and man, the man Christ Jesus (1 Tim. 2:5).

Jesus saith unto him, I am the way, the truth, and the life; no man cometh unto the Father but by me (John 14:6).

My little children, these things write I unto you, that ye sin not and if any man sin, we have an advocate with the Father, Jesus Christ the righteous: And he is the propitiation for our sins and not for ours only, but also for the sins of the whole world (1 John 2:1-2).

An individual does not have to be a Bible scholar to detect major differences between what God's Word says and what the Church of Rome, through Liguori, says. Much of the work attributed to Mary in *The Glories of Mary*, is actually work God has given His Son to do.

Because of the manmade teaching concerning Mary as "Mediatrix," it has been necessary for the Roman Catholic Church to present a convoluted view of God the Father and our Lord. Here are some examples, again from *The Glories of Mary*:

If God is angry with a sinner, and Mary takes him under her protection, she withholds the avenging arm of her Son, and saves him (124).

O Immaculate Virgin, prevent thy beloved Son, who is irritated by our sins, from abandoning us to the power of the devil (248).

We often obtain more promptly what we ask by calling on the name of Mary, than by invoking that of Jesus (248).

Liguori presents this imaginary scene: A burdened sinner sees two ladders ascending to heaven. At the head of one is Jesus; at the head of the other is Mary. As he tries to climb the ladder at which Jesus stands, he sees the angry face of the Lord and fails. As he turns away he hears a voice saying, "Try the other ladder." He does and climbs easily, meeting Mary at the top. She in turn brings him to heaven and presents him to her Son. Does that resemble at all the biblical picture of our Lord who said, "Come unto me, all ye that labour and are heavy laden, and I will give you rest. Take my yoke upon you, and learn of me; for I am meek and lowly in heart: and ye shall find rest unto your souls. For my yoke is easy, and my burden is light" (Matt. 11:28-30)?

Now we will notice some examples that Liguori gives from the lives and experiences of various individuals that support the uniquely Catholic view of Mary—her attributes and powers. Judge for yourself their veracity. In the first chapter of Volume 1, under the sub-heading, "Mary is the Mother of penitent sinners" this example is presented:

The Jesuit Father, Carlo Bovio, relates that in the year 1430 a young nobleman named Ernest gave all his patrimony to the poor and entered a monastery at Chateauroux in France. There he led such a holy life that his superiors came to think a great deal of him. They admired particularly his devotion to the Blessed Virgin. About that time a violent plague swept the city and the citizens came to the monastery for help. The abbot ordered Ernest to go and pray before Mary's altar and to stay there until the Madonna answered him. After three days he received an answer from Mary to the effect that certain prayers should be said. This was done and the plague ceased.

After a time, Ernest cooled in his devotion to Mary. The devil attacked him with many temptations. He was tempted particularly to impurity and to flee from the monastery. Since he had stopped praying to Mary, he yielded to the temptation and made plans to run away by climbing over the monastery wall. On his way out through the corridor, he passed in front of a statue of the Madonna. Mary called out to him and said: "My son, why are you leaving me?" Ernest was stunned at this, threw himself on the ground, and replied: "But, Mother, don't you see that I can't resist any longer? Why don't you help me?"

Our Lady answered; "Why didn't you come to me for help? Had you come to me, I would not have let you fall so low. From now on, call on me for help and don't be afraid of anything."

Ernest returned to his cell. His temptations returned, and again he failed to pray to Mary. Finally he fled from the monastery and gave himself over to a life of sin. Eventually he turned to murder. He took over the ownership of an inn where at night he would rob and kill poor travelers. One night he killed the cousin of the local magistrate. He was caught and sentenced to death.

Before he was taken into custody, however, another young guest arrived at the inn. Ernest made his usual plans to murder and rob the victim. But that night, when he entered the guest's room, he did not find the young man. In his place lay our crucified Savior, bleeding and covered with wounds. Jesus looked at him and said reproachfully: "My son, are you not satisfied that I died for you once? Do you want to kill me again? Very well! Raise your hand and strike!" Filled with remorse, the poor wretch began to cry and promised immediately to return to the monastery.

On his way he was overtaken by the police and freely admitted all his crimes. He was condemned to be hanged immediately, with no opportunity for confession. It was then that he once more thought of Mary and prayed to her for help. Mary heard his prayer. She personally loosened the noose around his neck and sent him back to the monastery. "Go back to the monastery," she said, "and do penance. And when you see a paper in my hands announcing your pardon, prepare to die." (42-43)

Such a "true life" example is used by Liguori to demonstrate the truthfulness of the Catholic position that "Mary is the Mother of penitent sinners."

In the third chapter of Volume 1, under the sub-heading, "Mary is the hope of sinners," this example is presented:

Blessed John Herolt, the Dominican scholar who out of humility called himself merely the "Disciple," tells the story of a married man who lived at enmity with God. His wife was unable to get him away from sin, but she begged him at least to practice some devotion to Mary even though he continued to live in sin. She suggested that every time he passed before a picture or statue of Mary he would greet her with a Hail Mary. The man began to practice this devotion.

One night, as he was on his way to commit a sin, he saw a light and noticed that it was burning before a statue of Mary holding the Infant Jesus in her arms. He said his usual Ave and then, to his amazement, he saw the Infant covered with wounds that oozed fresh blood. Frightened by this, the sinner began to realize that it was his own sins that had wounded his Redeemer. He broke into tears but noticed that the infant turned His back on him. He became alarmed. He turned his glance to Mary and said to her: "O Mother of mercy, your Son rejects me. Where can I find a more compassionate and powerful advocate than you? O my Queen, help me and pray for me!" Mary answered him and said: "You sinners call me the Mother of mercy, but at the same time you insist upon making me a Mother of sorrows by renewing my afflictions and the sufferings of my Son."

Nevertheless, she now turned to her Son and begged Him to pardon the sinner. Jesus continued to show Himself, as it were, reluctant to forgive. The Blessed Virgin then placed the Infant in the altar niche and knelt down before Him. "My Son," she said, "I will not leave here until you pardon this sinner." Then Jesus said to His Mother: "Mother, I cannot refuse you anything. Do you really want him pardoned? If you do, for the love of you I will pardon him. Make him come and kiss my wounds."

The sinner approached and kissed the Infant's feet. At once those wounds were healed. Finally, Jesus embraced him as a sign that He had forgiven him (77-78).

Another "true life" example by Liguori, this time meant to demonstrate that when all hope is lost, Mary is the hope for sinners. Imagine Jesus, who willingly gave His life on the cross for those who were so unworthy, being reluctant to forgive an obedient, penitent sinner. Imagine Jesus having to be convinced by Mary to forgive. Ligouri would have done well to study and meditate upon Romans 5:6-8.

We will look at just one more example. In the fifth chapter of Volume 1, under the sub-heading, "Mary's intercession is necessary for our salvation," this example is presented:

Both Vincent of Beauvais and Caesarius tell the following story. A certain noble youth, as a result of his vices, had been reduced to extreme poverty, so much so that he had to go begging. Confused and ashamed, the lad left his home town and took off for a distant city. On the way he met one of his father's former servants. Observing the young man's pitiable condition, he promised to lead him to a wealthy benefactor who would give him all the help he needed.

The servant happened to be a sorcerer. He took the youth to a lake in the middle of a forest and began to speak to some invisible person. When the lad inquired to whom he was speaking, the servant replied: "I am speaking to the devil." The boy was frightened but the servant continued his colloquy with the demon. "This young man," he said, "has lost everything and would like to be restored to his former position." The devil answered: "If he is ready to obey me, I shall make him even richer than before. But first, he must deny God."

The youth was horrified. But the servant continued to argue and cajole and finally the poor lad agreed and denied his Creator. The devil, however, was not satisfied. "You must also deny Mary," he said, "because Mary is our greatest enemy. See how many souls she snatches from our hands and leads back to God." "Absolutely not," answered the young man. "Mary I will never deny. She is my Mother, my life and my hope. I would rather spend the rest of my life as a beggar." With these words he left the place.

As he continued on his way, he passed a church dedicated to the Blessed Virgin. Tormented and troubled, he went in and knelt down before a statue of Mary. He begged Mary to intercede for him.

Is it true that the Son of God, who gave His life in the greatest manifestation of love that the world has ever known, is reluctant to forgive? Is it true that He must be begged and pleaded with by His Mother to do that for which He came?

Suddenly Mary appeared and began to pray for him. At first her divine Son said, "But Mother, this ingrate has denied Me." Mary continued to pray, and finally Jesus said: "Mother I have never refused you anything. Let the boy be pardoned, since that is what you ask of Me."

The man who had come into possession of the lad's fortune happened to be a witness of this entire scene. Touched by Mary's mercy, the man offered him his daughter in marriage and made him his heir. In this way Mary became the cause of his spiritual as well as his material rehabilitation (101-102).

This is another "true life" story which is supposed to show Jesus' reluctance to forgive, and the theory that Mary's intercession is necessary to salvation. Such as these "examples" that we have seen are the best proofs that can be offered to substantiate the peculiar tenets of Roman Catholic Mariology.

It is interesting to me that in the editor's preface to Volume 1 we find this statement, "Some of the stories and legends the saint narrates pertain, it is true, to an age and culture quite different from ours. But the lesson behind the stories is still practical and valid, and for that reason the original examples have been retained."

Is it true that the Son of God, who gave His life in the greatest manifestation of love that the world has ever known, is reluctant to forgive? Is it true that He must be begged and pleaded with by His Mother to do that for which He came? The lessons behind these examples do not teach practical or valid lessons. They present a perverted picture of our Lord and blaspheme His holy name. Yet these are the types of things presented in a "great work of Catholic Mariology," in a "masterpiece" by "Saint" Ligouri, a Doctor of the Roman Catholic Church.

I believe that Loraine Boettner, in his book, *Roman Catholicism*, aptly states the result of the Roman Catholic teaching that presents Mary as the "Mediatrix" when he writes:

> What a travesty it is on Scripture truth to teach that Christ demands justice, but that Mary will extend mercy! How dishonoring it is to Christ to teach that He is lacking in pity and compassion for His people, and that He must be persuaded to that end by His mother! When He was on earth it was never necessary for anyone to persuade Him to be compassionate. Rather, when He saw the blind and the lame, the afflicted and hungry, He was "moved with compassion" for them and lifted them out of their distress. He had immediate mercy on the wicked but penitent thief on the cross, and there was no need for intercession by Mary although she was there present. His love for us is as great as when He was on earth; His heart is as tender; and we need no other inter-mediary, neither His mother after the flesh, nor any saint or angel, to entreat Him on our behalf (147-148).

Mary is not honored by creating doctrines that give her positions of power and influence that God did not give her. Indeed, to do so besmirches the simple biblical picture of the humble, faithful mother of Jesus.

The Inquisition

If you were raised as a Roman Catholic and attended parochial schools for the first twelve years of your education, chances are good that you have heard very little about the Inquisition, or perhaps nothing at all. The Inquisition is a historical event that the Roman Catholic hierarchy would like to forget. It is practically ignored in Catholic high school histories, and when the subject is addressed in question and answer columns in Catholic papers and periodicals, it is very briefly explained away. A classic example of what I am talking about occurred in *The Question Box* column of May 10, 1956. Here are the question and answer. The answer is by Rev. J. V. Sheridan, a Catholic priest:

> Question: As a potential convert I am interested in some specific information (not mere generalities) on the real and official attitude of the Catholic Church towards non-Catholics, as well as a comment on the following questions: (1) "Does your church claim, or has she ever claimed, the right to punish or persecute dissenters such as lapsed Catholics, Protestants, or non-religionists?" (2) If your reply is in the negative, how can you explain the frightful atrocities of the Inquisition or the harshness of the Church today in Italy and Spain toward Protestants?

> Answer: (1) The Church does not claim, nor has she ever claimed the right to punish or persecute religious dissenters because of their beliefs. Her concept of faith as a gift from God and not the mere product of fear, force or theological research should be sufficient proof of this statement. (2) Underlying many of the customs and laws of countries like Spain and Italy is the Catholic philosophy of life. The ordinary citizenry (*not the church*) formed in such a philosophy is bound to react harshly against the intrusions of those whose subjectivistic theology, if not outrightly anti-Catholic, endorses divorce, contraception and euthanasia—ideas that are repugnant to traditional Christian doctrine and discipline.

As you can see, there is no explanation given of the Inquisition, no admittance of wrong. Actually, the impression was given that what did occur in the Inquisition was the result of the outrage of good Catholic people. When the truth is known, good Catholic people recoil in horror at what their Church, led by the infallible popes, did in the name of God. Let's examine the historical development of this dark time in history and perhaps we can understand why this major event is left out of, or barely mentioned in, Catholic history textbooks.

What Does It Mean?

The name "inquisition" is derived from the Latin *inquirere* (to inquire) and it "signifies the form of procedure used, that of searching out heretics and other offenders instead of waiting for charges to be made" according to the *Encyclopedia Americana* (XV: 191). Bear in mind that the heretics referred to were heretics as far as Roman Catholic doctrine was concerned. This Inquisitional procedure is of utmost importance because it lies at the heart of the Inquisition and reveals much about the nature and character of it. Let's allow *The New Catholic Encyclopedia* (VII: 537), describe the procedure for us. You can draw your own conclusion as to the fairness of it and whether or not it was something that Jesus would have condoned:

> The Inquisitorial procedure was a departure from the traditional forms of accusation or of denunciation, *which had been ill suited to the repression of heresy.* According to the new procedure the judge could, ex officio, bring suit against any individual who might even *vaguely* be the object of public rumor. The inquisitus became his own accuser. When questioned on the charges brought against him, he was obliged to take an oath to tell the truth. . . .This judicial process, which in time became normal, underwent a number of modifications as a result of various apostolic constitutions, especially those of Gregory IX, Innocent IV, and Alexander IV. *The accused did not know the witnesses for the prosecution and was thus deprived of any opportunity to challenge and confront them.* This precaution can be explained by the need to protect informers from reprisals by relatives and friends of the accused. Faced by nameless accusers, the defendant's only recourse was to reveal the names of his principle enemies. *Factors that normally disqualified a witness from testifying were eliminated: testimony was accepted from criminals, infamous persons, the excommunicated, and heretics.* It was even considered an obligation for heretics to become informers. *Blood relationship did not dispense one from testifying.* Lawyers and clerks, moreover, were not able to offer their services to the accused, for they would then become accomplices.

This description of the inquisitorial procedure is from the pages of an authorized Roman Catholic source; it was not made up by those who are the enemies of Catholicism or by someone seeking to discredit that religious body. This method, or procedure of "inquiry," was the heart of the Inquisition. All people, and especially Roman Catholics, need to know how this procedure grew into the full-blown institution of the Inquisition that it became. A good question to consider as we look at its historical development is, "How did a church guided by an 'infallible' leader (and heresy is certainly within the realm of faith and morals) institute and sanction such an unholy thing as the Inquisition?"

How and Why It Began

As early as the eleventh century we can read of "heretics" being put to death by secular rulers, and it appears that, at that time, the Catholic Church did not officially support such actions. However, by the middle of the twelfth century, Catharism and other heresies had spread so rapidly that Henry II of England and Louis VII of France pressed Pope Alexander III to take strong steps against heretics. He agreed, and in 1163, at the Council of Tours, he commanded the clergy to search out heretics. Heretics were considered to be enemies of the human race, and this was the first general papal legislation against heresy.

The hierarchy didn't respond too energetically to this command, and heresy continued to flourish. In 1179 Alexander issued stronger commands concerning heretics at the Third Lateran Council.

Even more severe was the legislation of Pope Lucius III from Verona on November 4, 1184. Pope Innocent III pushed the purge of heresy even further, authorizing a crusade against the Albigensians of southern France in 1207-1208. The Fourth Lateran Council of 1215 confirmed previous measures and commanded secular princes to assist. Pope Innocent III considered the heretic to be guilty of "spiritual treason." The importance of that point is this: If civil treason was punishable by death, how much more severe a punishment did treason against Jesus Christ deserve?

However, it was Emperor Frederick II who, in 1224, legislated that the impenitent, heretical Cathari of northern Italy should die by fire as punishment for their heresy. Here is a quote from the *Encyclopedia Americana* (XV: 192):

> In 1231, Pope Gregory IX adopted the imperial legislation, and from 1231 to 1235 he formally established and defined the procedures of the medieval

Inquisition. Abandoning the use of special legations, the Pope sent first Dominicans and then Franciscans to establish the Inquisition in France. In 1235 he named Robert le Bougre as inquisitor for the entire realm. . . .The same pattern was soon extended to Germany, northern Italy, and Spain, usually at the request of the secular authority. It was, therefore, Gregory IX who established the Inquisition as a papal tribunal appointed to suppress heresy through procedures established in Roman Catholic canon law: inquisition haereticue pravitatis.

The Inquisition continued to grow throughout the Middle Ages. In 1252 Pope Innocent IV authorized the use of torture by the Inquisition. In the latter part of the Middle Ages, the Inquisition was taken over by the civil authorities.

Perhaps the most infamous of all was the Spanish Inquisition. Responding to the request of the Catholic monarchs, Ferdinand and Isabella, on November 1, 1497, Pope Sixtus IV established the Inquisition in Castile, giving the monarchs the right to appoint the inquisitors with Rome retaining the right of approval. In October of 1483, Tomas de Torquemada was appointed Inquisitor General of Spain and his appointment was approved by the papacy. The Inquisition was abolished in Spain in 1808 by Joseph Bonaparte.

There is another very interesting fact about the Inquisition and the attitude that allowed it to develop. In 1542 Pope Paul III established the Roman and Universal Inquisition, or the Holy Office. This tribunal is probably most noted for its persecution of Galileo in 1633. However, on December 7, 1695, this "Holy Office" was changed to the Congregation for the Doctrine for Faith and Morals. It is still in existence today.

The Inquisition was a dark time in the history of man. It was not the result of the outcry of the people. It was organized and sanctioned by Rome—by the various popes, the infallible vicars of Christ on earth. Why is it virtually ignored by Catholic teachers and authorities? Why do they attempt to just explain it away?

I now want to quote rather extensively from the *Encyclopedia Americana* (XV: 195) so that we can understand and appreciate what happened during the Inquisition, and so we can get a feel for the type of terror it prompted among the common people. The following would have been the normal operating procedure of the Inquisition during the thirteenth century:

> Arriving at a town or village, the inquisitor convoked clergy and people to a solemn assembly. There he delivered a sermon touching upon the evils of

heresy and summoned the guilty to voluntary confession of their crimes. . . .
Following the solemn assembly and its summons to confession and repentance,
a period of grace ranging between 15 and 30 days was allowed. Those who
appeared, confessed their guilt, and abjured their errors were treated lightly.
With the expiration of the period of grace, the inquisitor then demanded that
the faithful denounce those suspected of heresy and, with the aid of reliable
members of the community, began a systematic search for suspects. The sworn
testimony of two witnesses sufficed to commit the accused to prison, where
hunger, lack of sleep, and various constraints gradually reduced his will to resist. Summoned before the tribunal, the accused was told of his alleged crimes,
*but he was never confronted by those who had laid the charges. . . . The accused was
not allowed any legal defense, a practice justified by the ingenious argument that if
the accused was innocent he had nothing to fear, and therefore he had no need of
a defender.* If he was guilty, it was the duty of his advocate to persuade him to
admit his guilt. Any advocate so foolish as to attempt to genuinely defend the
accused would be rendered infamous. . . .Defenseless, then, the accused confronted the tribunal. There followed a subtle interrogation by the inquisitor.
The Inquisition soon found these devices insufficient. Torture was practiced by
the civil tribunals of the Middle Ages, and in 1252 Pope Innocent IV authorized its use by the Inquisition.

Punishments — Sentences For the Guilty

Now let us suppose that an individual was found guilty of heresy. What
would happen to him or her? Again we find the answer in the *Encyclopedia
Americana* (XV: 195):

> The interrogation concluded, the inquisitor now sought to reach a judgment
> by scrutinizing all records and consulting his advisors. . . .The decisions of
> the Inquisition were then made public in a solemn religious ceremony. Held
> always on a Sunday, it began with a procession of the ecclesiastical and civil
> dignitaries and the accused. The latter were often dressed in special costume.
> The procession provided the assembled populace with a striking display of pag-
> eantry and religious observance that veiled but thinly the grim seriousness of
> the occasion.

> Following a sermon, the decisions of the Inquisition were read out, public
> abjurations were received, and sentences were pronounced. All sentences were
> final; there are only a few recorded instances of an appeal to Rome. (Even *The
> New Catholic Encyclopedia* supports this with the following statement, "The
> right to appeal to the Apostolic See was denied by the constitution Excommu-
> nicamus of Gregory IX" [VII: 537].) The sentences ranged from light ones—
> fines, the wearing of distinctive costumes for a stated period of time, penances,
> pilgrimages, the assumption of the crusader's cross, infamy (with its attendant

civil disabilities), and flagellation to the most terrible. For convicted heretics who abjured their crimes, the customary punishment was *imprisonment for life*. (Of prison life for these unfortunates, the *New Catholic Encyclopedia* [VII: 539] says, "The prison's diet consisted of the 'bread of sorrow and the water of tribulation,' but certain prisoners were allowed supplementary food. The usual imprisonment was at least tolerable for the incarcerated; but strict immuration, i.e., murus strictus, involved solitary confinement, with no regard to health.") For the convicted and impenitent, as well as for those who had relapsed into their former errors, the practice was to abandon them to the secular arm with a prayer for moderation in inflicting mutilation or death. The formula was pure fiction, designed to absolve the church from participation in the shedding of blood. After the conclusion of the ceremony, these unfortunates were burned to death in a place reserved for these executions, *a punishment sanctioned by church and state and approved by the learned and the holy*. Those who abjured at the stake were often strangled before the fire was lighted, a small concession to humanity. Those executed or condemned to life imprisonment were deprived of goods and property, *thus condemning their descendants to a life of penury*. The arm of the Inquisition reached even into the grave. The bodies of those convicted of heresy posthumously were exhumed and burned. The goods of their descendants were confiscated.

What Happened to the Confiscated Goods?

What about the goods of those found guilty that were confiscated? What happened to them? *The New Catholic Encyclopedia* tells us, "A portion of the confiscated property was payable to the inquisitors. In Italy, as early as the time of Innocent IV, this portion was set at one-third of the total." In almost all instances, the inquisitors were Roman Catholic authorities.

How Many Died?

Just how many people died as a result of the work of the Roman Catholic inquisitors? The *Encyclopedia Americana*, (XXVI: 863) tells us this of the Inquisitor General of Spain, Torquemada, "During his term of office, tens of thousands were hauled before its courts and at least 2,000 perished at the stake." From the book, *The Age of Faith*, Will Durant writes, "Compared with the persecutions of heresy in Europe from 1227 to 1492, the persecution of Christians by Romans in the first three centuries after Christ was a mild and humane procedure."

Really, though, it is not important for us to know the exact number of those murdered in the Inquisition. The fact that any died by the authority of a man claiming to be the Vicar of Christ on earth, the representative of Him who died for all men and who said, "Father, forgive them for they know not what they do," as He hung on the cross, is almost outside the realm of belief. It does no good to excuse it by saying it was a product of the times or to seek to justify it on the basis of its historical context. It was, and is, inexcusable, and it renders the claim of infallibility and the claim of being the one true Church ridiculous.

Catholic Views of Prominent Figures of the Inquisition

Our examination has shown the Inquisition to have been a reprehensible event, worthy only of condemnation. When trying to find an official Catholic position concerning what took place during the Inquisition, one will find it labeled as "indefensible." *The New Catholic Encyclopedia* says quite plainly, "But even when Roman, Byzantine, and emerging national legal precedents are recalled and when due consideration is given to the manipulation of this tribunal for reasons of state, the excesses attendant upon its procedures, especially in southern France and in Spain, make the Inquisition, *as it evolved in practice*, indefensible."

That is a noble admission and one with which we would agree. However, upon closer examination, we find that *The New Catholic Encyclopedia* did not tell the whole story. Perhaps we can better tell how the Catholic hierarchy views the Inquisition by determining how they view some of those people who were prominent in the Inquisition itself, or those who set forth the principles that allowed the Inquisition to develop. How do they view some of those responsible for putting those principles into bloody practice?

Thomas Aquinas

The most authoritative philosopher and theologian of the Roman Catholic Church of all time was Thomas Aquinas. He was a Dominican and is still held in the highest possible esteem. Again, according to *The New Catholic Encyclopedia*, (XIV: 109), "In 1918, St. Thomas became an institution in the Church with his being mentioned in the *Code of Canon Law*—this is the only name in the Code—with the injunction that the priests of the Catholic Church *should receive their philosophical and theological instructions 'according to the method, doctrine and principles of the Angelic Doctor.'*" As a matter of fact, Pope Leo XIII, in describing the influence of Aquinas on the Council of Trent, said, "The Fathers of Trent, in order to proceed in an orderly fashion during the conclave, desired to have opened upon the altar, together with the Scriptures and the decrees of the supreme pontiffs, the *Summa* of St. Thomas Aquinas *whence they could draw council, reasons and answers*" (XIV: 110).

A summary of how the Catholic Church feels about Thomas Aquinas is found once again in *The New Catholic Encyclopedia*. It says:

> And the Church approves him before all others because in his writings, as in no others, the totality of truth has found a unique expression, an expression of exemplary value. Thomas himself professed no doctrinal particularity; he belonged to no school; he was content with no existing synthesis. He undertook, rather, the grandiose project of choosing everything, of seeking the deeper intentions of an Aristotle and of an Augustine, of probing the ultimate meaning of both human reason and divine faith. He knew the limitations of human minds, his own included. And yet he searched for a wisdom that would incorporate and transcend all earthly knowledge, confident that such wisdom was to be found in the bosom of his Church. *With reason, perhaps, that same Church finds in him the outstanding exemplar of the Catholic saint and scholar, and has never hesitated to recommend his study to her children.*

These are truly marvelous words of praise for a prominent Catholic theologian and prominent figure behind the principles of the Inquisition. How did this "exemplar of the Catholic saint and scholar" view the Inquisition? Aquinas wrote, "Though heretics must not be tolerated because they deserve it, we must bear with them, till, by a second admonition, remain obstinate in their errors, must not only be excommunicated, but they must be delivered to the secular power to be exterminated" (*Summa Theologica*, IV: 90; cited by Loraine Boettner in *Roman Catholicism, 425*).

Aquinas wasn't done. Again in *Summa Theologica* (II: 154), he wrote, "So far as heretics are concerned, heresy is a sin, whereby they deserve not only to be separated from the church by excommunication, *but also to be severed from the world by death.*" He also wrote, "If counterfeiters of money or other criminals are justly delivered over to death forthwith by the secular authorities, much more can heretics, after they are convicted of heresy, be not only forthwith excommunicated, but as surely *put to death*" (II, Q. 2, Art. 3).

How can the Catholic Church call the Inquisition "indefensible" and then turn around and call a man who taught the very principles that allowed it to happen, "the outstanding exemplar of the Catholic saint and scholar"? In an encyclopedia published in 1966 it was written, "the church approved him before all others because in his writings, as in no others the *totality of truth* has found a unique expression." Was it the right of the Catholic Church to have people put to death because they did not agree with them, to confiscate their property, to imprison them for life, part of the "totality of truth"? How can they call it "indefensible" yet raise to such a high position one who defended it?

Ignatius Loyola

Another prominent and authoritative voice of Roman Catholicism heard during the time of the Inquisition and still greatly esteemed today was Ignatius Loyola, founder of the Jesuits. About him *The New Catholic Encyclopedia* (VII: 351) says:

> St. Ignatius, who so often received visits from the Lord, always kept to himself his nostalgia for the luminous abysses of the Trinity; but he knew he had been chosen more to *transmit the divine light* than to enjoy it. God called him to the work of redemption, to the service of the Lord in the establishment of the kingdom. Thus he chose to be a soldier under the standard of the cross. Above, and at the same time the source of both contemplation and action, there is "love." However, though loving action often demands that one renounce the pleasures of contemplation, these are not lost without compensation in the holy gifts and spiritual favors from the Lord. *Such a spirituality reminds one of St. Paul, the apostle of the Gentiles,* "urged by a love of Christ" and living in the intimacy of the Spirit.

Again we see marvelous words of praise and commendation for a prominent thinker, teacher, and worker–Ignatius Loyola, founder of the Jesuits.

Here is what "St." Ignatius, who reminded the writers of *The New Catholic Encyclopedia* so much of Paul and who lived in the "intimacy of the spirit" according to them, had to say about heretics and the punishment of them as practiced in the Inquisition:

> It would be greatly advantageous, too, not to permit anyone infected with heresy to continue in the government, particularly the supreme government, of any province or town, or in any judicial or honorary position. Finally, if it could be set forth, and made manifest to all, that the moment a man is convicted or held in grave suspicion of heresy he must not be favored with honors and wealth but put down from these benefits. And if a few examples could be made, *punishing a few with the penalty of their lives, or with the loss of property and exile,* so there could be no mistake about the seriousness of the business of religion, this remedy would be so much more effective *(Obras Completas de San Ignacio de Loyola,* Translated by Dwight Cristoanos; Madrid; 1952; 880 p.; Cited by Loraine Boettner in *Roman Catholicism).*

Why call the Inquisition "indefensible" and then canonize an individual who advocated those very same "indefensible" things, even comparing him to the Apostle Paul?

Torquemada

The Spanish Inquisition has the reputation of having been extremely vicious. We discussed earlier the Grand Inquisitor General of Spain, Torquemada, and that at least 2,000 died as a result of his efforts.

As hard as it is to believe, *The New Catholic Encyclopedia* (VII: 540) defends this man: "'Legend' has transformed Torquemada into a cruel monster, but he was actually an energetic, uncouth religious, utterly devoid of ambition, who succeeded in giving his own austere character to the new institution."

Torquemada was not just "an energetic, uncouth religious." Two thousand people, at least, were burned at the stake during his reign. Why defend a man who played a major role in the "indefensible" action and institution?

Ferdinand III

The Spanish king, Ferdinand III, so pleased the Roman Catholic Church by his vigorous and vicious actions against heretics that he was made a saint in 1671 and had words of praise for him inserted into the Breviary (a book of daily readings and prayers for the priests). This is what the Breviary says, "He permitted no heretics to dwell in his kingdom, and with his own hands brought wood to the stake for their burning" (*The Stability and Progress of Dogma*, Cardinal Lepicier, 202 [1910]. Cited by Loraine Boettner in *Roman Catholicism*, 428). Why call the Inquisition "indefensible" in a book that the public might very well read, and then praise an inquisitor for his killing of heretics in a book commonly read only by Roman Catholic priests? It does make an interesting question.

Is It Really "Indefensible"?

During his consecration, every Roman Catholic bishop takes an oath of allegiance to the Pope. Contained within this oath is the following: "With all my *power I shall persecute and make war upon all heretics, schismatics and those who rebel against our Lord (the Pope) and all his successors. . . .* So help me God and these the holy gospels of God" (*Pontificale Romanum Summorum Pontificum*, Belgium, Mechlin, 133; cited by Emmett McLoughlin, *American Culture & Catholic Schools*). Just what is the official position of the Catholic hierarchy concerning the Inquisition? It certainly seems inconsistent to condemn the institution and then praise those who nurtured it and were part of it.

How does such conduct compare with the words of our Lord where He said, "But I say to you, love your enemies, bless those who curse you, do good to those who hate you, and pray for those who spitefully use you and perse-cute you, that you may be sons of your Father who is in heaven; for He makes His sun rise on the evil and on the good, and sends rain on the just and on the unjust" (Matt. 5:44-45)?

The Spirit of the Inquisition in Modern Times

Up to this point we have looked at the Inquisition of the twelfth, thir-teenth, fourteenth, and fifteenth centuries. There is a tendency to dismiss these things as having happened years ago and to feel that certainly things are much different now. To do so would be to make a grave mistake, for the spirit of the Inquisition existed well into the twentieth century and continues to exist today in under-developed Catholic countries. It is with a certain de-gree of trepidation that I write this, for I realize that most American Roman Catholics will find these things hard to believe. However, an honest examina-tion demands it.

Just One Case–Cardinal Alojzije Stepinac

The events that we are about to detail took place before, during, and after the Second World War. They are not ancient history. Let us allow *The New Catholic Encyclopedia* to introduce us to Cardinal Stepinac.

Alojzije Stepinac was born in Croatia (which was later to become part of Yugoslavia) on May 8, 1898. Picking up in *The New Catholic Encyclopedia* we read:

> In 1924 he enrolled in the German College, Rome, and attended classes at the Gregorian University. In 1930 he obtained doctorates in philosophy and the-ology and was ordained. Returning to Zagreb (1931), he was assigned to the chancery office. He became coadjutor (May 1934), then archbishop (Decem-ber 1937), of Zagreb, the largest see in Yugoslavia. As archbishop, he promoted Catholic charities and Catholic Action, defended the Church's rights, and de-nounced Communism and National Socialism. In April 1941, he welcomed the Croatian State, *but continuously opposed the regime of Ante Pavelic, especially for its forced conversions and racial persecution. Thousands of the persecuted Jews, Slovenes, and Serbs received his help.* . . .He was arrested in September 1946; *was tried on trumped-up charges of collaborating with the Ustashi regime, Germans, and Italians; and on October 11 was sentenced to 16 years of imprisonment.* . . . Pius XII named him cardinal (December 1952). . . .The U.S. Congress and the free world hailed him as a martyr for faith and freedom. Several high schools and church auditoriums in the U.S. were named after him (702-703).

That which *The New Catholic Encyclopedia* tells us of Cardinal Stepinac presents him as quite an impressive fellow, a dedicated servant of the Catholic Church, a martyr for the faith, a persecuted prisoner, and a champion of freedom. The dates in the encyclopedia are accurate, but that is about all. As we examine the other side of Cardinal Stepinac's life and work, ask yourself why these things were not presented in *The New Catholic Encyclopedia*, an authorized Catholic work bearing the Imprimatur, thereby purporting to be free of error.

The Other Side

The following information can be found in *The Vatican Against Europe*, written in 1959 by Edmond Paris, who happened to have been born a Roman Catholic; in *Genocide in Satellite Croatia*, also written by Edmond Paris in 1959 (both books completely and fully documented); in *Assassins in the Name of God*, by Herve Lauriere; and in *Roman Catholicism*, by Loraine Boettner. Here is what happened.

After World War I, Yugoslavia was formed by the uniting of the Roman Catholic states of Croatia and Slovenia with the Eastern Orthodox state of Serbia. Immediately the Croats began to plot against the Serbs with terrorist *Ustashi* bands being formed. These particular groups were supported by Mussolini. In 1934 the king of Yugoslavia, Alexander I, was assassinated in France. The leader of the assassins was Ante Pavelic (remember his name, for it was his later regime that *The New Catholic Encyclopedia* claimed Stepinac opposed). Pavelic was given protection by Mussolini even though both French and Yugoslav officials had convicted him of this crime.

Roman Catholicism details the following chain of events:

When in 1941 the Nazis invaded Yugoslavia the Croats, with Pavelic as their leader, joined them. As a reward Hitler made Pavelic the puppet head of the new "Independent State of Croatia." His minister of religion was Andrija Artukovic, another Roman Catholic. Then began a war of suppression or extermination of all Serbs and Jews. Nearly 70,000 of the 80,000 Jews in the new state were killed or forced to flee, *their property being confiscated. Official records and photographs show that Pavelic and Archbishop Stepinac were closely associated in governmental, social and ecclesiastical affairs. Stepinac was appointed supreme military apostolic vicar of the Ustashi army led by Pavelic* (436).

These facts, supported by official records and photographs, do not indicate that Cardinal Stepinac, "continuously opposed the regime of Ante Pavelic" as

The New Catholic Encyclopedia told us. However, this is just the beginning. Again from *Roman Catholicism* we read:

> In May, 1941, after innumerable massacres had been committed, *Pavelic went to Rome and was received by Pope Pius XII. . . .*In June of that year more than 100,000 Orthodox Serbian men, women, and children were killed by the Ustashi (over whom Stepinac was supreme military apostolic vicar—g.l.). In all, some 250 Orthodox churches were destroyed or *turned over to the Roman Catholic parishes and convents. Documents requesting and authorizing such transfers are now in the state prosecutor's office at Zagreb and Sarajevo, bearing the signature of Archbishop Stepinac. In February 1942, a Te Deum was sung in Stepinac's church in Zagreb, the then capital of Croatia, with special honors paid to Pavelic. In a pastoral letter Stepinac declared that in spite of complexities, what they were seeing in Croatia was "the Lord's work," and called on his priests to support Pavelic. Stepinac twice visited Pope Pius XII in Rome in 1942. He reported that 244,000 Serbs had accepted (forced) conversion to Roman Catholicism. So the pope, too, was well informed as to what was going on in Serbia and Croatia.* (436).

When the Nazis were forced to retreat from Yugoslavia, Pavelic and Artukovic, along with almost all the Roman Catholic priests, went with them. Yugoslav courts found Cardinal Stepinac guilty of Nazi-Fascist collaboration, and he was sentenced to sixteen years of imprisonment. He served five years and was then released under house arrest by Tito. How did the Roman Catholic hierarchy react to these crimes? Pope Pius XII named him a cardinal in 1952, and Cardinal Spellman of New York named a high school after him.

This was an episode as cruel and as full of mystery as anything that took place in the Inquisition of the Middle Ages. Why doesn't the Catholic hierarchy simply admit it instead of covering it up, or worse yet, misrepresenting the facts? Could it be that the American Roman Catholic laity would not stand for it if they knew? Unfortunately, most Catholics have heard nothing, or very little, about the blackest spot in their history known as the Inquisition. But be assured that the spirit of the Inquisition lives where the people and the government will allow it.

The Papacy

Without question the single most visible symbol of Roman Catholicism to the world is the pope. Roman Catholics look to him as the infallible guide in all matters of religion. His position is set forth in the following manner in *The Catechism of the Catholic Church*: "The Pope, Bishop of Rome and Peter's successor, is the perpetual and visible source and foundation of the unity both of the bishops and of the whole company of the faithful. For the Roman Pontiff, by reason of his office as Vicar of Christ, and as pastor of the entire Church has full, supreme, and universal power over the whole Church, a power which he can always exercise unhindered" (234). Perhaps only events involving the royal family of Britain are characterized by such pageantry and ceremony as are the public appearances of the Roman Pontiff. The extent of his influence is seen in his "full, supreme, and universal power over the whole company of the faithful," and the Roman Catholic Church is by far the largest body of people on earth who claim to worship Christ.

Did the Papacy Begin With Peter?

Roman Catholics are taught that the papacy began with Peter, the apostle. Again, from *The Catechism of the Catholic Church* we find, "The Lord made Simon alone, whom he named Peter, the 'rock' of his Church. He gave him the keys of his Church and instituted him shepherd of the whole flock" (233).

In *A Catechism of Christian Doctrine* (Revised Edition of the *Baltimore Catechism #3*), the following question and answer appear: "Did Christ give special power in His Church to any of the apostles?" "Christ gave special power in His Church to Saint Peter by making him the head of the apostles and the chief teacher and ruler of the entire church. (a) The power of the keys was promised to Saint Peter and was actually conferred on him. (b) Saint Peter was recognized by the early Christians from the beginning as the head of the church" (III: 111).

The primary passage of Scripture given to support these statements is found in Matthew 16:13-19. The passage reads as follows:

> When Jesus came into the coasts of Caesarea Philippi, he asked his disciples, saying, Whom do men say that I the Son of man am? And they said, Some say that thou art John the Baptist; some, Elias; and others, Jeremias, or one of the prophets. He saith unto them, But whom say ye that I am? And Simon Peter answered and said, Thou art the Christ, the Son of the living God. And Jesus answered and said unto him, Blessed art thou, Simon Barjona: for flesh and blood hath not revealed it unto thee, but my Father which is in heaven. And I say also unto thee, That thou art Peter, and upon this rock I will build my church; and the gates of hell shall not prevail against it. And I will give unto thee the keys of the kingdom of heaven: and whatsoever thou shalt bind on earth shall be bound in heaven: and whatsoever thou shalt loose on earth shall be loosed in heaven.

If we move just one page further in *A Catechism of Christian Doctrine*, we find this question and answer:

> Did Christ intend that the special power of chief teacher and ruler of the entire church should be exercised by Saint Peter alone?

> Christ did not intend that the special power of chief teacher and ruler of the entire church should be exercised by Saint Peter alone, but intended that this power should be passed down to his successor, the Pope, the Bishop of Rome, who is the Vicar of Christ on earth and the visible head of the Church. (a) A successor to Saint Peter, the first bishop of Rome, was required as chief teacher and ruler for the same reason that successors were required for the other apostles. From the very beginning it was acknowledged by the Church that the successor of Saint Peter as Bishop of Rome was at the same time the head of the entire Church. This successor of Saint Peter is called the Pope (112).

As a product of the parochial school system, this is what I was taught. It is what all Roman Catholics are taught. However, it is simply not true, and history, from both secular sources and sources claimed by the Roman Catholic Church itself, conclusively proves that it is not.

I find it fascinating, and more than a bit revealing, that there is no absolute, unquestioned biblical evidence to support the idea that Peter ever resided in Rome. When Paul wrote his letter to the Romans in late A.D. 57 or early A.D. 58, there is no mention of Peter. Twenty-six members of the church in Rome are mentioned by name, but not Peter. When Paul was a prisoner in Rome, there is no indication that Peter was there. "Only Luke is with me" is what Paul wrote in 2 Timothy 4:11. While this does not prove that Peter was absent from Rome at that time, it does make one wonder why, if he was there, he had deserted the imprisoned Paul. Also, in Peter's letters, he makes no mention of Rome. In his salutation of 1 Peter 5:13, he wrote, "The church that is at Babylon, elected together with you, saluteth you; and so doth Marcus my son." There is no reason to assume that Babylon is symbolically referring to Rome at this time. There was a Babylon in both Egypt and Assyria when Peter wrote this letter. Even the noted scholar, Philip Schaff, in his comments concerning 1 Peter 5:13, wrote, "The Jewish population in Babylon at this time was considerable; so many historians have rightly held Babylon in this passage to be literal Babylon of Assyria."

Even informed Roman Catholic scholars admit that any biblical evidence of Peter actually being in Rome is extremely weak. Karl Keating, president and founder of Catholic Answers and the author of the best selling book *Catholicism And Fundamentalism*, wrote, "In any event, let us be generous and admit that it is easy for an opponent of Catholicism to think, in good faith, that Peter was never in Rome, at least if he bases his conclusion on the Bible alone. But restricting his inquiry to the Bible is something he should not do, external evidence has to be considered, too" (201). The external evidence to which Keating refers is not nearly as strong as I would personally like it to be if I were going to base such an important doctrine as Peter being the first Pope, Vicar of Christ on earth and Bishop of the universal Church, upon it.

Our attention now turns to the Scriptures. Whenever Roman Catholic authorities speak of the papacy, the passage most often used by them in its defense is Matthew 16:18. Those twenty-nine words have been used as the starting point for what has grown to be the massive organization of the Roman Catholic Church. Due to the importance placed upon this particular verse by the Roman Catholics, it is important for Catholics and non-Catholics alike to know exactly what it says and the use made of it by those who believe in the primacy of Peter.

Let us notice, once again, Matthew 16:18: "And I say also unto thee, That thou art Peter, and upon this rock I will build my church; and the gates of hell shall not prevail against it."

As we begin our examination of Matthew 16:18, the source that I will be using to present the Roman Catholic teaching concerning it will be *The Question Box*, by Bertrand L. Conway. It bears the Nihil Obstat (meaning "Nothing stands in the way") and the Imprimatur (meaning "Let it be printed").

On page 148 this question is asked, "Does not the rock mean Christ (Matt. 16:18) as we read in the Bible 'and that rock was Christ' (1 Cor. 10:4)?"

Conway begins his answer by saying, "In Matt. 16:18 the word 'rock' refers to Saint Peter as many fair-minded Protestant commentators admit. . . ."

On page 150, this question is asked, "Does not the use of the two words, *Petros* and *Petra*, (Matt. 16:18) prove a clear difference in meaning?"

Conway's answer was, "Not at all. Our Lord did not speak Greek, but Aramaic, which uses the same word, *Kepha*, in both places. Saint John tells us Peter's name, Cephas, was equivalent to *Petros* (John 1:42)."

It is important to realize that in Matthew 16:18, *petros* is the word used for Peter, while *petra* is the word translated "rock." Do these two words prove a clear difference in meaning as the question asked, or do they support the Catholic position that the two words refer to the same thing?

According to *Vine's Expository Dictionary of New Testament Words*, the comments concerning *petra* are as follows: "Denotes a massive rock, as distinct from *petros*, a detached stone or boulder, or a stone that might be thrown or easily moved. . . .In Matt. 16:18, metaphorically, of Christ and the testimony concerning him; here the distinction between *petra* concerning the Lord himself, and *petros*, the apostle, is clear."

Conway, as is consistent with all Roman Catholic scholars, makes a major point out of the fact that Jesus spoke Aramaic, a language that would use the same word in both instances. However, Matthew, writing under the inspiration of the Holy Spirit, wrote in Greek, a language that does allow for the distinction between the two. Evidently the Holy Spirit saw fit for Matthew to make the distinction clear. *Petra* and *petros* do not refer to the same thing.

At this point we should mention that Roman Catholic scholars persist in the claim that Matthew originally wrote his gospel in Aramaic and that the Greek gospel of Matthew was simply a translation. They base this assertion upon a questionable quotation of Papias in *Eusebius' Ecclesiastical History*, in which he was alleged to have written, "Matthew composed his history in the Hebrew dialect (probably Syro-Chaldaic, sometimes called Hebrew, g.l.), and every one translated it as he was able" (3, 39, 14).

Roman Catholic authorities continue to make this assertion in spite of considerable evidence to the contrary. *The International Standard Bible Encyclopedia* says, "One thing which seems certain is that whatever this Heb. (Aram.) document may have been it was not an original form from which the present Gr. Gospel of Mt. was translated, either by the apostle himself, or by somebody else. . . .Indeed, the Greek Matthew throughout bears the impress of being not a translation at all, but as having been originally written in the Greek. . ." (III: 2010).

The *Zondervan Pictorial Encyclopedia of the Bible* says, "It must be admitted, however, that no fragment of an Aram. Matthew has ever been found and a Greek edition is more plausible than a Greek translation. Matthew's gospel does not give evidence of being a translation, which is one of the weak evidences for the Aram. theory" (IV, #124).

Conway also mentioned that John tells us that Peter's name, Cephas, was equivalent to *petros* in John 1:42. He is absolutely correct and that just serves to prove our point. *Thayer's Greek-English Lexicon of the New Testament*, tells us that *petros* means "stone." So *petra* (the rock) denotes a great, immovable mass of rock; while *petros* denotes a detached stone or boulder. These are two completely different things.

As is typical of so much of the Roman Catholic reasoning, Conway launches into a bit of circular logic. We have already noted that he wrote, "The word rock refers to Saint Peter." However, in *The Question Box* we find this question, "Do not the early Fathers speak of Peter's faith as the rock? Does not Saint Augustine state that the rock is the confession Peter made? Do not others declare that the rock is Christ?" (150).

Here is Conway's answer. "None of these interpretations deny that Peter is the rock foundation of the Church, as we have explained. Taken together they make the true meaning all the more clear. Christ is the original Rock on which Peter rests; Peter is the Rock or foundation of the Church. Faith is the

Rock of the Church, i.e., Peter's faith is that which makes him the foundation of the Church. Peter's confession is the rock inasmuch as his profession of Christ's divinity merited him the honor of being made the foundation of the Church."

Despite the fact that Peter and his confession cannot both be the rock, and grammatically they do not refer to the same thing, this reasoning adds yet another foundation. The truth is, the rock is the fact that Jesus is the Christ, "the son of the living God." Simply adhering to what the Bible says removes all question. "For other foundation can no man lay than that is laid, which is Jesus Christ" (1 Cor. 3:11). "And are built upon the foundation of the apostles and prophets, Jesus Christ himself being the chief corner stone" (Eph. 2:20).

Steps Toward Papacy

For more than the first 500 years of the church there was no such thing as one man presiding in Rome as the universal bishop of the Church. To be sure, there were bishops in Rome over those years who sought supremacy for themselves and Rome, the most notable of which would be Leo I (440-461). He succeeded in getting Emperor Valentinian III to issue an edict declaring the Roman See as the supreme court of appeal for all bishops (*Encyclopedia Britannica*, 489-492). However, when one considers the fact that such an edict was even necessary it becomes readily apparent that the Roman bishop (which is in itself a departure from the biblical pattern) was not recognized as the universal bishop as late as the fifth century A.D.

Even as certain Roman bishops were making these strides toward power, opposition was widespread and strong. Cyprian, bishop of Carthage from A.D. 246-258, said in his *Epistle LXIX*, "None of us has ever dared to proclaim himself bishop of bishops, forcing with tyrannical terror the obedience of his colleagues."

So strong was the opposition that even Augustine, today held as a champion of Roman Catholicism, when he was acting as secretary at the Council of Carthage in A.D. 430 wrote, "Anyone who appeals to those overseas (this would be Rome—g.l.), shall not be received by the communion of the bishops of Africa" (*The Bible vs. Romanism*). These are very stern words indeed. It does not require much research to determine that the statement, "From the *very beginning* it was acknowledge *by the Church* that the successor of Saint Peter as Bishop of Rome was at the same time the head of the entire Church" is at best highly misleading and at worst blatantly false.

The Roman Catholic Church places a great deal of importance upon the writings of what they called the "Early Church Fathers." The writing of the Ante-Nicene Fathers, many of whom are regarded as having been Catholics by the Roman Church, are filled with statements indicating that no one man, including Peter, was at any time viewed as the Vicar of Christ on earth and the universal bishop of the church.

Tertullian, who admittedly held some heretical views in the latter years of his life, wrote in the early part of the third century, "Just, for example, as if Peter too had censured Paul, because whilst forbidding circumcision, he actually circumcised Timothy himself. Never mind those who pass sentence on apostles. It is a happy fact that Peter is on the same level with Paul" (*On Prescription Against Heretics*, XXIV).

Origen, another third century writer who is called by *The Catholic Encyclopedia*, "a priest" and an instructor of many Roman Catholic "saints" wrote in his *Commentary on Matthew*:

> And perhaps that which Simon Peter answered and said, 'Thou art the Christ, the Son of the living God,' if we say it as Peter, not by flesh and blood revealing it unto us, but by the light from the Father in heaven shining in our heart, we too become as Peter, being pronounced blessed as he was, because that the grounds on which he was pronounced blessed apply also to us, by reason of the fact that flesh and blood have not revealed to us with regard to Jesus that He is Christ, the Son of the living God, but the Father in heaven,...And if we too have said like Peter, 'Thou art the Christ, the Son of the living God,' not as if flesh and blood had revealed it unto us, but by light from the Father in heaven having shone in our heart, we become a Peter, and to us there might be said by the Word, 'Thou art Peter,' etc. For a rock is every disciple of Christ of whom those drank who drank of the spiritual rock which followed them, and upon every such rock is built every word of the church (10).

In the same commentary, Origen wrote:

> But if you suppose that upon that one Peter only the whole church is built by God, what would you say about John the son of thunder or each one of the Apostles? Shall we otherwise dare to say, that against Peter in particular the gates of Hades shall not prevail, but that they shall prevail against the other Apostles and the perfect? Does not the saying previously made, 'The gates of Hades shall not prevail against it,' hold in regard to all and in the case of each of them? And also the saying, 'Upon this rock I will build my church'? For in this place these words seem to be addressed as to Peter only, 'Whatsoever thou shall bind on earth shall be bound in heaven,' etc; but in the Gospel of John

the Saviour having given the Holy Spirit unto the disciples by breathing upon them said, 'Receive ye the Holy Spirit' (11).

Cyprian, writing in the mid third century, in his *Epistle LXX*, wrote, "For neither did Peter, whom first the Lord chose, and upon whom He built His Church, when Paul disputed with him afterwards about circumcision, claim anything to himself insolently, nor arrogantly assume anything; so as to say that he held the primacy, and that he ought rather to be obeyed by novices and those lately come" (3).

Truly, on and on we could go with quote after quote from the Ante-Nicene Fathers that clearly indicate that the idea of one universal bishop, Vicar of Christ on earth, presiding in Rome as the Father of the Faithful, was unknown to the early Church. The earliest usage of the word "pope", "papa" in Latin, that can be found was by Dionysius of Alexandria, some time between A.D. 200-265, in his *Epistle VII – To Philemon, a Presbyter*, in which he refers to "our Blessed *Father* Heraclus," who was his predecessor at Alexandria. It is apparent that this term came to be applied to all bishops, and signified no preeminence in those who bore it.

The first person to assume the title of "Pope" as universal bishop, was not even in Rome. It was John, bishop of Constantinople, in A.D. 588.

The first person to assume the title of "Pope" as universal bishop, was not even in Rome. It was John, bishop of Constantinople, in A.D. 588. In response to this, Gregory I, bishop of Rome and later called Gregory the Great and recognized by Rome as one of the greatest of Popes, wrote to him in *The Bible vs. Romanism*:

> You know it, my brother; hath not the venerable council of Chalcedon conferred the honorary title of universal upon the bishops of this apostolic See, whereof I am, by God's Will, the servant? And yet none of us hath permitted this title to be given him; none has assumed this bold title, lest by assuming a special episcopate, we should seem to refuse it to all the brethren. . . .But far from Christians be this blasphemous name by which all honor is taken from all other priests, while it is foolishly arrogated by one (67).

Gregory the Great was not done. To the emperor, Mauritius, he wrote, "I am bold to say, that whosoever adopts or affects the title of universal bishop has the pride and character of anti-Christ, and is in some manner his forerunner in this haughty quality of elevating himself above the rest of his order" (*The Bible vs. Romanism*, Trice, 68). These are words from the man recognized by most Roman Catholic scholars as a primary architect of the modern papacy.

Later, the extremely wicked Emperor Phocas applied the title of Pope as universal bishop to this same Gregory in A.D. 604. According to Malachi Martin in *The Decline and Fall of the Roman Church*, this was a man who had "beheaded each of his predecessor's five sons, then put out Mauritius' eyes (this was his predecessor), and after torture, disemboweled him" (80). Malachi Martin was a former Jesuit professor who served in Rome with Cardinal Augustine Bea and Pope John XXIII. Gregory refused the title, but it was later assumed by Boniface III in A.D. 607. Even then it was a mere "court title" and certainly not recognized universally by the Roman Church, even as it passed down to his successors, until the days of Charlemagne and the Holy Roman Empire.

I have presented all of this simply to demonstrate that the papacy did not spring from the mind of God and it did not start with Peter. Such statements as we saw earlier, "From the very beginning it was acknowledged by the Church that the successor of Saint Peter as Bishop of Rome was at the same time head of the entire Church" are just not true. They are blatantly false. History shows that the papacy grew in the minds of ambitious men and bears no resemblance to what Jesus promised to build, His Church.

Papal Infallibility

Reasonable people understand that men make mistakes. We all say and do things from time to time that are wrong and sinful. Christians believe that there has been only one perfect man in the history of mankind, Jesus Christ our Lord. Because of this we are inclined to overlook shortcomings in individuals, realizing that they are, after all, only human. But there is one man who cannot be viewed so charitably due to the claims made by him and for him. That man is the Pope. From *Pastor Aeternus* by Pius IX we read:

> The Roman Pontiff, when he speaks *ex-cathedra*, that is, when, in discharge of the office of pastor and teacher of all Christians, by virtue of his supreme Apostolic authority he defines a doctrine regarding faith and morals to be held by the Universal Church, is, by divine assistance promised him in Blessed Peter, possessed of that infallibility with which the divine Redeemer willed that His Church should be endowed in defining doctrine regarding faith and morals.

So reads the document setting forth the Roman Catholic teaching concerning Papal Infallibility. As a product of the parochial school system I was taught that this doctrine was implied in the Bible, that it had always been accepted by Roman Catholics the world over, and that it was merely confirmed as an ancient dogma of the church by the Vatican Council of 1870 with complete unanimity. What a shock it was to find that *none* of what I was taught concerning this subject was true!

Pius IX went on to declare that Papal Infallibility was "a tradition received from the beginning of the Christian faith." Indeed, if the doctrine was to carry any weight at all, it had to be retroactive. The problem is that the early Roman Catholic Church had no such tradition, and neither did a large portion of the church as late as 1870. Dr. Geddes MacGregor says in his book, *The Vatican Revolution*:

> In spite of the early recognition of the importance of the See of Rome and the consequent prestige of its bishop, there is not even a hint of an *ex cathedra* notion before the eleventh century. Even in the fourteenth, in the lively debates on the nature of papal pronouncements, no such common notion was being either combated or upheld (137).

In *What Rome Teaches*, a booklet by Edward J. Tanis, we find this statement:

> Gregory the Great was one of the most powerful and influential popes, bishop of the congregation in Rome from 590 to 604. He made a large contribution to the improvement of the preaching and music of the church and was an ardent defender of the Catholic traditions, but Gregory never taught that he was the infallible head of the whole church. Foakes-Jackson, the scholarly historian, quotes Gregory the Great as saying that the title of pope as 'Ecumenical Bishop' (bishop of the whole church) was "proud and foolish" and "an imitation of the devil" (17).

Another very interesting point must be considered if papal infallibility was a "tradition received from the beginning of the Christian faith." In Keenan's *A Doctrinal Catechism*, a Roman Catholic catechism in use before 1870, we find this question and answer:

> "Must not Catholics believe the pope himself to be infallible?" "This is a protestant invention; it is no article of the Catholic faith; no decision of his can oblige, under pain of heresy, unless it is received and enforced by the teaching body, that is, the bishops of the church."

After 1870, the year in which the doctrine of papal infallibility was defined and decreed, this question and answer was simply omitted. There was no explanation as to why. In a debate that took place in Cincinnati, Ohio, on January 13, 1837, between Archbishop Purcell and Alexander Campbell, Purcell stated:

> Appeals were lodged before the bishop of Rome, though he was not believed to be infallible. Neither is he now. No enlightened Catholic holds the pope's infallibility to be an article of faith. I do not; and none of my brethren that I know of do. The Catholic believes the pope, as a man, to be as liable to error, as almost any other man in the universe. Man is man, and no man is infallible, either in doctrine or morals (*Debate on the Roman Catholic Religion*, Campbell & Purcell, 27).

So we can see that this doctrine was not something always believed by the church. Why was it that the teachers I trusted while growing up, and Catholic authorities today, continue to teach that it was?

Unanimous Confirmation

Catholics are taught that this doctrine was confirmed by the unanimous consent of those at the Vatican Council of 1870. That is not the whole story. In the first place, the vote was 533 affirmative, two negative, and 106 absent. That is not unanimous and still doesn't tell the whole story.

Twenty-seven North American bishops, including Purcell of Cincinnati, Kendrick of St. Louis, McCloskey of New York, forty-six German and Austrian bishops, and forty-one French bishops sent letters to Pius IX before the Council asking that infallibility be removed from the agenda. On the day before the vote was to be taken, eighty-eight bishops left Rome because they could not in good conscience vote for something *they did not believe in* and if they stayed and voted negatively, there would be papal reprisals to contend with.

Certainly most Roman Catholic laymen would be shocked to learn that this supposed "unanimously" approved doctrine was opposed by the bishops and archbishops of Paris, Prague, Vienna, Rottenburg, Mainz, Orleans, Marseilles, Grenoble, Besancon, Dijon, La Rochelle, Halifax, Cincinnati, St. Louis, Pittsburgh, Savannah, Wheeling, Newark, Little Rock, New York, and a host of others. All of this information is available in *American Culture & Catholic Schools* by Emmett McLoughlin (117-118) and in *Under Orders* by William Sullivan.

In addition to this evidence of a lack of unanimity, a group of Roman Catholic anti-infallibilists met in Munich, Germany in September, 1871, and withdrew from the Roman Catholic Church. They formed what is known as the "Old Catholic" Church, and it continues to this day. They constitute living proof that Rome's claim of unanimity of consent concerning infallibility is simply not true.

Implied in the Bible?

In Roman Catholicism, individual Bible study is not emphasized; consequently, the majority of the laity knows very little about God's Word. So when the church authorities declare something to be implied in the Scriptures, few Catholics are in a position to know whether it is or isn't. Most (and I know, for I was one of them) will simply accept what the clergy says. Here is how the infallibility of the Pope, as successor of Peter is said to be implied. In *A Course in Religion for Catholic High Schools and Academies* by John Laux, M.A., we find:

> Infallibility does not depend upon the virtue or the learning of the Pope, but on the special assistance of the Holy Ghost, given him according to the promise of Christ, who said to Peter: "I have prayed for thee that thy faith fail not; and then, being once converted, confirm thy brethren."
>
> Hence in defining the Infallibility of the Successor of Saint Peter, the Vatican Council did not introduce a new doctrine, but simply defined— i.e., solemnly declared in precise words—the ordinary and normal mode in which Christ willed and provided that His Church should be kept infallibly in the path of Divine truth and saved from the assaults of her foes (97).

History clearly shows that many of the "infallible" popes made grievous errors in their teaching concerning "faith and morals."

In making such a statement the Roman Catholic authorities make it appear that Peter never made a mistake in matters of "divine truth" after the church began and that his successor, through the same help of the Holy Spirit, will not either. A quick glance at Galatians 2:11-14 will show that Peter was not infallible. He made a mistake in a matter of faith and Paul said he was to be blamed. That destroys any basis for saying that the Bible implies papal infallibility.

History clearly shows that many of the "infallible" popes made grievous errors in their teaching concerning "faith and morals." As we examine a number of errors we should bear in mind that it will do no good to dismiss them with "the pope was not speaking *ex cathedra*." Supposedly the whole point of papal infallibility was to preserve the church from error in matters of faith and morals and Roman Catholics are officially required to accept all the teaching of the pope "in obedience to the authority of the Pope and in respect for his wisdom" (*A Catechism of Christian Doctrine*, Revised Edition of the *Baltimore Catechism*, 128). So what are Catholics to do when the Pope teaches error because he was not teaching *ex cathedra* when they are bound to accept all that he teaches? It has become clear that the whole *ex cathedra* idea was invented to take care of just the kind of papal errors that we are going to look at.

Mistakes of the Popes

Pope Vigilinus (538-555): According to *History of the Christian Councils*, by Hefele, Pope Vigilinus would not condemn a number of heretical teachers during the heated monophysite controversy and he actually refused to attend the fifth Ecumenical Council at Constantinople of 553. The Council went ahead without him and threatened him with excommunication. In response, Vigilinus, an "infallible pope," submitted to the opinions of the Council and confessed that he had been a tool of Satan.

Pope Gregory the Great (590-604): Gregory wrote to the Emperor Mauritius that anyone who would take the title of Universal Bishop had the "pride and character of *anti-Christ*" (*The Bible vs. Romanism*, 67-68). But **Boniface III** took the title of Universal Bishop in 607, and it has been worn by the popes since. Which of the "infallible popes" was wrong—Gregory or Boniface?

Honorius (625-638): In *Fundamental Protestant Doctrines II*, we read:

> The greatest scandal of this nature is Pope Honorius. He specifically taught the Monothelite heresy in two letters to the patriarch of Constantinople (that is, that Christ had only one will, which by implication meant that he denied either His deity or His humanity). The opinion was condemned by the sixth ecumenical council (680) which condemned and excommunicated Honorius by name (Honorio haeretico anathema, Session XVI) (13).

Here was a supposedly "infallible pope" branded a heretic for teaching something opposed to the Roman Catholic faith. How can that be?

Hadrian II (867-872): Hadrian stated that civil marriages were valid. But **Pius VII** (1800-1823) stated that civil marriages were invalid. Which "infallible" pope was right?

Eugene IV (1431-1447): Eugene declared Joan of Arc to be a witch and condemned her to be burned alive. **Benedict XV** in 1919 declared her a saint.

That decree was 488 years too late for Joan, but which "infallible" pope was right?

Clement XIV issued a decree on July 21, 1773, suppressing the Jesuit Order. On August 7, 1814, **Pius VII** issued a decree restoring them. It is difficult to harmonize two such contradictory decrees by two "infallible" men when the decrees both deal with the same subject.

It was difficult for me, as a Catholic, to accept these facts, but that is what they are—facts. A classic case of the absurdity of the claim of papal infallibility is presented in *Ins and Outs of Romanism*. Dr. Zacchello said:

> Were popes Paul V (1605-1621) and Urban VIII (1623-1644) infallible when they condemned Galileo for holding a true scientific theory? Did they not declare the Copernican theory was false, heretical, and contrary to the word of God? Did they not torture and imprison Galileo in the dungeons of the Inquisition for not sharing their erroneous views? In their decree prohibiting the book of Copernicus, *De Revolutionibus*, the congregation of the index, March 5, 1619, denounced the new system of the mobility of the earth and immobility of the sun as "utterly contrary to the Holy Scriptures."

Now it is very easy to see that Pope Paul V and Pope Urban VIII considered this to be in the area of faith, an area in which they were supposed to be infallible. They condemned the theory on the basis that it was heretical and "utterly contrary to the Holy Scriptures." They were wrong, clearly so. What does that do to the theory of papal infallibility? I am aware of the fact that more recently even Pope John Paul II felt compelled to clear Galileo, but why didn't he simply and openly explain how an "infallible" pope could be mistaken in the area of faith?

The vast majority of Roman Catholics do not know these instances of papal fallibility. They accept what the clergy tells them and they won't hear these things from a priest.

"By Their Fruits Ye Shall Know Them"
Of the Pope, the *New York Catechism* says:

> The pope takes the place of *Jesus Christ on earth*... by divine right the pope has supreme and full power in *faith and morals* over each and every pastor and his flock. He is the true *Vicar of Christ*, the head of the entire church, the father and *teacher* of all Christians. He is the infallible ruler, the founder of dogmas, the author of and the judge of councils; the *universal ruler of truth*, the arbiter of the world, *the supreme judge of heaven and earth*, the judge of all, being judged by no one, *God himself on earth.*

The *New York Catechism* is not saying anything that the popes themselves have not said. In his encyclical, *The Reunion of Christendom* (1885), Pope Leo XII stated that the pope holds "upon this earth the place of God Almighty." Such statements and claims lead us to believe that the popes must indeed be extraordinary people. They are, and have been "God himself on earth," according to the infallible teaching of the Roman Catholic Church, and everyone knows that God can do no sin. This is what I believed as a child growing up in Catholicism. It was the logical conclusion of what I was taught. At that time I did not know the true history of some of the popes or the theological attempts to explain away their actions.

Our Lord Jesus said, "Wherefore by their fruits ye shall know them" (Matt. 7:20). Let's see what kind of fruit some of the past popes bore in their lives.

Pope Stephen VII (896-897): According to Michael Walsh in *An Illustrated History of the Popes,* this "Vicar of Christ" treated the dead body of a predecessor, Formosus, in an absolutely inhumane manner. He had the body exhumed after it had been buried for nine months, dressed in papal vestments, and placed on trial. Dead Formosus was found guilty of ambition and Pope Stephen annulled all of Formosus' actions as pope, had his fingers cut off, possibly beheaded the corpse, and threw what was left in the Tiber River.

Pope Sergius III (904-911): In *History of the Popes*, Ludwig Pastor writes that this "supreme judge of heaven and earth" lived with a prostitute named Marozia and her daughter. He had a son by Marozia and this son later became pope.

Pope John XI (931-935): Here was the illegitimate son of Sergius III and Marozia. About this "father and teacher of all Christians," Cardinal Baronius said in his *AANALES*, *"The Holy Roman Church has been vilely corrupted by a monster like him."*

Pope John XII (955-963): As "infallible ruler," "he was ordained at eighteen, and looked on the papacy as a means of enjoying life to the full. He ordained to the priesthood his companions of the stable; his chief pleasures were women and hunting; his ignorance was startling even to his contemporaries in an age not noted for its learning. John XII was deposed for his immorality, and scorned for his bad grammar" (*An Illustrated History of the Popes*, 93).

Pope Benedict IX (1033-1045): According to the *Encyclopedia Brittanica* (XIX: 497), he was made the "universal ruler of truth" at the tender age of twelve. Soon he was disgracing the office with every form of excess until he finally sold the office of pope in order to win the hand of a lady.

The list goes on and on. During the Renaissance there was the infamous Rodrigo de Borja, Pope Alexander VI. This particular "arbiter of the world" had ten illegitimate children by four different mistresses and is thought to have gained office in the first place through bribery (*An Illustrated History of the Popes*, 145).

There is much more evidence just like the evidence we have seen. We would readily expect the Catholic Church to have some sort of explanation for the actions of these men and why it does not destroy their claims for the papacy, and they do. All can judge the validity of their explanation for themselves. In *What the Church Teaches*, a question and answer book by J.D. Conway and bearing the Imprimatur of Ralph L. Hayes, Episcopus Davenportensis, this statement is made:

> Infallibility does not keep the Pope from sin. It does not depend on the moral-
> ity or the intelligence of the man, but is inherent in the office… It does not
> keep him from personal error in matters of doctrine and morality; it only keeps
> him from leading the Church into error in this area.

The Catholic Church is saying that they have never taught that the Pope could not sin; and they never have said so in so many words. But when you call a man Bishop of Rome, Vicar of Jesus Christ, Successor to the Prince of the Apostles, Supreme Pontiff of the Universal Church, Patriarch of the West, Primate of Italy, Archbishop and Metropolitan of the Province of Rome, Sovereign of the Vatican City, Servant of the Servants of God, father and teacher of all Christians, infallible ruler, founder of dogmas, author of and judge of councils, universal ruler of truth, arbiter of the world, supreme judge of heaven and earth, judge of all, and finally, God Himself on earth, what are you implying? If such a one is not perfect, if he sins as do all the rest of us, then how can he dare to assume the title Vicar of Christ, and even worse, God himself on earth?

The history of some of the popes proves that all of the powers and titles claimed for and by the office of the papacy are just not valid. Even if only one pope had been immoral, if only one had sinned, the claims of being the Vicar of Christ and God Himself on earth would be destroyed. As it is, many were actually vile men and their claims cannot be accepted.

The Roman Catholic Priesthood

Probably the most readily identifiable feature of the Roman Catholic Church to the everyday man and woman is the priesthood. Almost everybody who has any age on him at all has seen the old Bing Crosby movie, "The Bells of St. Mary," in which he played a priest. Almost everyone at some time or another has come across a man wearing a Roman collar, the kind that looks as if he has the collar of his shirt turned around. Practically everyone has heard something about the celibacy of the Roman Catholic priesthood. So we will look at what the priesthood consists of, how one becomes a priest, what (if any) special effects or powers come with the priesthood, and whether or not there is any authority for the whole thing to exist in the first place.

Holy Orders

The term that is used to describe the rite of ordination into the priesthood is "Holy Orders." *The Baltimore Catechism* defines Holy Orders in the following manner:

> Holy Orders is the sacrament through which men receive the power and grace to perform the sacred duties of bishops, priests, and other ministers of the Church. The distinction between clergy and laity is of divine origin, for first, Christ chose the twelve apostles from among His disciples; and in a special way deputed and consecrated them for the exercise of spiritual ministrations; and second, the apostles, who could not mistake the will of Christ, administered the sacrament

of Holy Orders by consecrating bishops and by ordaining priests and deacons (451).

So what we are talking about is a group of men, separate and apart from the rest of the people (or laity), who have certain special spiritual powers. These powers, coupled with the position these men hold in the Roman Catholic Church, serve to elevate them above the rest of their fellow Catholics. A good question to consider would be, "How does an individual become a priest?"

How Does One Become a Priest?

The Baltimore Catechism says the following about how a man becomes a priest:

> For a man to receive the sacrament of Holy Orders worthily, it is necessary first that he be in a state of grace and be of excellent character; second, that he have the prescribed age and learning; third, that he have the intention of devoting his life to the sacred ministry; fourth, that he be called to Holy Orders by his bishop. (b) Those who are called by God to be priests ordinarily receive no special revelation to this effect. God expects all to use the gifts of reason and of grace in determining their state of life. (c) Without a special dispensation no one may be ordained a priest until he is twenty-four years of age. Ordinarily the prescribed learning consists of four years of high school, four years of college, and four years of theology completed in a seminary. (d) The sacred ministry of the priesthood can be exercised either as a diocesan priest under a bishop, or as a member of a religious community under a religious superior. Priests of religious orders make the vows of poverty, chastity, and obedience. Diocesan priests bind themselves to chastity for life and make a solemn promise of obedience to their bishops.

During the course of these years of study, the men preparing for the priesthood go through a number of stages of advancement. The two major ones prior to the priesthood are "subdeacon" and "deacon." This is primarily what is involved as one makes his way toward ordination. We should mention, however, that due to a lack of vocations (or those choosing to become priests), the Roman Catholic Church has begun to waive some of those requirements. I am aware of a seminary in Boston for what is called a "late vocation." These are men a little older who have experienced life and decided to become priests. In those cases, if they are accepted, their learning and training consists of three years in the seminary.

Special Effects or Powers

The Baltimore Catechism says, "The effects of ordination to the priesthood are: first, an increase of sanctifying grace; second, sacramental grace, through which the priest has God's constant help in his sacred ministry; third, a character, lasting forever, which is a special sharing in the priesthood of Christ and which give the priest special supernatural powers." The catechism also states, "The chief supernatural powers of the priest are: to change bread and wine into the body and blood of Christ in the Holy Sacrifice of the Mass, and to forgive sins in the sacrament of Penance." Those are the special effects and supernatural powers that go with being a priest in the Roman Catholic Church.

The ability to change bread and wine into the body and blood of Christ is called "Transubstantiation," which we will study in a later chapter. The second chief supernatural power mentioned is said to be the ability to forgive sins. This particular practice of Roman Catholicism is called "Auricular Confession." It is part of the sacrament of Penance and is called "auricular" because, generally speaking, the sins are whispered privately into the ear of a priest. This takes place in a small booth called a "confessional." This is beginning to change somewhat, and the strictness of the little confessional is beginning to be relaxed, but the power to forgive sins still rests solely with the priest.

The Roman Catholic authorities use a few scriptures to make their case. One such scripture is James 5:16, which says, "Confess your faults one to another, and pray for one another, that ye may be healed. The effectual fervent prayer of a righteous man availeth much." Roman Catholic authorities interpret that passage as though it said, "Confess your faults to a priest," but it does not say that. The true import of that passage is that of Christians mutually confessing sins to one another after said sins have been confessed to God. There is no foundation in this passage for confession, privately, to a specially ordained priest for the purpose of forgiveness.

The most frequently used passage is found in John 20:22-23, which says, "And when he had said this, he breathed on them, and saith unto them, Receive ye the Holy Ghost. Whosoever sins ye remit, they are remitted unto them: and whosoever sins ye retain, they are retained." The contention of Roman Catholicism is that this passage gives ordained priests the power from God to forgive sins that are confessed to them. But this passage does not deal with confession of sins and a priest's power and prerogative to forgive them or not to forgive them. This power has nothing to do with private confession to a priest. The apostles were commissioned to preach the gospel of Jesus Christ. When people heard, believed, repented, confessed their faith in Jesus, and were baptized for the remission of their sins, they then had their sins remitted. If they rejected the gospel, refusing to believe and obey, their sins were retained. Only in this sense did the apostles possess the authority to forgive or retain sins, and all who would teach anyone the gospel of Christ has the same power—the gospel.

Consider this—if the apostles had had the power to forgive sins, then Peter's statement in Acts 8:22 to Simon the sorcerer would have been unnecessary. He said, "Repent therefore of this thy wickedness, and pray God if perhaps the thought of thine heart may be forgiven thee." Peter could have given him absolution himself if he had possessed the power that Catholic priests are supposed to have.

What Is the Laity?

Within Roman Catholicism there is a clear and rigid distinction between its people. One group is known as clerics, or the "clergy," while the other is referred to as the "laity." *The New Code of Canon Law* is quite specific about these groupings. In Canon 207-1 it is explained this way: "Among the Christian faithful by divine institution there exist in the Church sacred ministers, who are also called clerics in law, and other Christian faithful, who are called laity."

As would be expected, these two groups have decidedly different functions and rights. The laity consists of the common people, the man and the woman in the pew. The clergy is made up of the priests, out of which group the holders of higher ecclesiastical offices are chosen. A casual reading of *The New Code of Canon Law* would seem to indicate that the laity also is eligible for ecclesiastical offices, giving them a voice in the decision-making process of the Roman Church. Canon 228-1 reads, "Qualified lay persons are capable of assuming from their sacred pastors those ecclesiastical offices and functions which they are able to exercise in accord with the prescriptions of law."

However, closer examination of the same *Code* shows that that is not the case. In order for a member of the laity to be appointed to an ecclesiastical office, he must be able to exercise the functions of that office in accord with the prescriptions of law. Well, the law effectively shuts them out. Canon 150 states, "An office entailing the full care of souls, for whose fulfillment the exercise of the priestly order is required, cannot be validly conferred upon someone who has not yet received priestly ordination."

So regardless of the language of Canon 228, no member of the laity can be appointed to an ecclesiastical office that would have any say concerning matters of faith or morals, for such obviously comes under the heading of "the full care of souls."

What, then, is the function of the laity as far as the Roman Catholic authorities are concerned? John L. McKenzie, S.J. (meaning that he is a member of the Society of Jesus—a Jesuit), explains what their function and place is in his book, *The Roman Catholic Church*, which bears the Imprimatur of Joseph P. O'Brien, S.T.D., Vicar General, Archdiocese of New York. McKenzie writes:

> In Roman Catholicism the laity are passive members of the church. If the work of the church is conceived in the usual threefold division of government, the sacramental system, and preaching, the laity are the governed, the recipients of the sacraments, and the listeners. Of course, the laity are not simply inactive, but the long tradition of church office and functions leaves no place in the structure for lay activity. . . .It will also appear that in Romanism ecclesiastical has become synonymous with clerical (82-83).

What, then, is the primary function of the laity as far as Roman Catholic authorities are concerned? Again, McKenzie supplies the answer from *The Roman Catholic Church* where he says, "The one activity which is steadily and seriously urged on the laity is the activity of supporting the economic structure of the Roman Church. This is not said cynically. The Church engages in a vast operation that demands proportionately vast resources of personal and plant" (83).

> **"The one activity which is steadily and seriously urged on the laity is the activity of supporting the economic structure of the Roman Church.**

I must confess to being surprised by the candor displayed by McKenzie, but he states the exact truth. The Roman Catholic laity is expected by their superiors to support financially the numerous projects of the Roman Church over, and in which, they have absolutely no say. Truly, theirs is not to reason why; theirs is but to foot the bill.

Having left the vast throng of the Roman Catholic laity and looking back, two things amaze me. One is the willingness of many fine, intelligent people to accept such a subservient position. The second is the audacity of the Roman Catholic authorities to both allow and to perpetuate the myth of a clergy-laity distinction. A fundamental principle of Romanism is that "no proposition can be declared an article of faith *unless perpetual belief in the church can be affirmed of it"* (*The Roman Catholic Church*, 212). In Canon 207 of *The New Code of Canon Law*, it is stated that the clergy-laity distinction is "by divine institution." The very ones who make that statement know that it is not true. Once again McKenzie tells us from his officially authorized book:

> When one compares the laity in the Roman Catholic Church with the laity in the New Testament church, or even with the laity in Protestant churches, especially those churches which are called congregational, some striking differences are apparent. *The New Testament does not exhibit that kind of clergy-laity polarity, which is seen in Roman Catholicism.* . . .The New Testament writings contain little which is addressed to the "clergy" (actually, it contains none—g.l.); neither *the word nor the idea as it has developed is found in the New Testament* (82).

There you have it from the pen of one of Roman Catholicism's own authorized writers and a member of its clergy. The word "clergy" is not found in relation to the early church, nor is the idea even implied. If perpetual belief in something by the church must be affirmed to be declared an article of faith, and it is admitted that the clergy-laity distinction was not part of the New Testament church, how can it then be called "by divine institution" in *The New Code of Canon Law* in 1983? The answer is that it cannot be, at least truthfully. But to correct it means to run the risk of losing the support for "the economic structure of the Roman Church."

The Clergy-Laity Distinction

If the priesthood and the clergy-laity distinction are taught in the Bible, then we must accept it. If God has set forth in His Holy Word all of these different requirements for a man to become a special minister to Him, then we must accept them. If God did promise to give the special effects and supernatural powers to a select group of people, then we must accept that fact. However, if the Word of God does not teach these things, then we must reject them immediately.

Let us begin with the existence of the priesthood in the first place. Does this exclusive group of people have any right to exist as a group, according to God's Word? Does the Bible truly teach the clergy-laity distinction, since we were told by *The Baltimore Catechism* that the clergy-laity distinction was of divine origin?

In 1 Peter 2:9, Peter wrote to Christians, specifically those scattered about Pontus, Galatia, Cappadocia, Asia, and Bithynia. He was writing to all of those Christians, young and old, men and women. In that particular verse

Peter wrote, "But ye are a chosen generation, a royal priesthood, a holy nation, a peculiar people; that ye should show forth the praises of him who hath called you out of darkness into his marvelous light." Peter referred to the entire group of Christians as "a royal priesthood." I fail to see a clergy-laity distinction there.

In Revelation 1:6, John was writing to the seven churches of Asia. Once again, these churches included young and old, men and women. Here he said, "And hath made us kings and priests unto God and his Father; to him be glory and dominion forever. Amen." In other words, all Christians are priests. Again, I fail to see a clergy-laity distinction there.

The peculiar office of the priesthood is an attempt to elevate certain men above their fellow men. It gives the man who is the priest a position of honor and reverence. Now, lest anyone would say that this is not the priest's fault but rather the fault of those who give him that honor, let's look at some of the Catholic teaching concerning the attitude the laity is to display toward those who are priests. In *The Baltimore Catechism* the following statement is made, "Catholics should show reverence and honor to the priest because he is the representative of Christ Himself and the dispenser of His mysteries. In showing reverence and honor to the priest one shows reverence and honor to Christ Himself, for the priest in a very true sense is 'another Christ.'"

The concept of a clergy-laity distinction with special "reverence and honor" due to the clergy is contrary to the entire tenor of New Testament teaching. Jesus taught:

> Ye know that the princes of the Gentiles exercise dominion over them, and they that are great exercise dominion over them, and they that are great exercise authority over them. But it shall not be so among you: but whosoever will be great among you, let him be your minister; and whosoever will be chief among you, let him be your servant: Even as the Son of man came not to be ministered unto, but to minister, and to give his life a ransom for many (Matt. 20:25-28).

We have already seen that the Bible teaches we are all priests if we have obeyed the gospel of Christ, and that we are all to work to the best of our ability in the service of Jesus. That includes study and preparation as Paul told Timothy with these words, "Study to show thyself approved unto God, a workman that needeth not to be ashamed, rightly dividing the word of truth" (2 Tim. 2:15). But all of the rules and regulations, such as age, being called by a bishop, and man-made educational requirements are not found in the

Scriptures. If they were, then certainly none of the early evangelists, with the possible exception of Paul, would have been qualified purely on the basis of education alone. A lot more time spent studying the Bible and recognizing the role of all Christians instead of years spent studying Catholic theology in a seminary would much better prepare a person to do the Lord's Work.

Titles

Did you know that in addition to the title, "Father," the proper way to address a bishop or archbishop is to call him "Your Excellency"? To address a cardinal properly, you are to call him "Your Eminence," and the Pope is called "Your Holiness." But Jesus said:

> But all their works they do for to be seen of men: they make broad their phylacteries, and enlarge the borders of their garments, and love the uppermost rooms at feasts, and the chief seats in the synagogues, and greetings in the markets, and to be called of men, Rabbi, Rabbi. But be not ye called Rabbi, for one is your Master, even Christ. But he that is great among you shall be your servant. And whosoever shall exalt himself shall be abased; and he that shall humble himself shall be exalted (Matt. 23:5-12).

This "honor and reverence" which the Roman Catholic authorities teach should be given to a certain group of men is not found in the Scriptures. In truth, it is completely contrary to what the Bible says.

Celibacy in the Roman Catholic Church

One of the best-known aspects of the Roman Catholic priesthood is its required celibacy. "Celibacy" is the requirement by the Roman Catholic Church that its priests and monks do not marry. It is not the same as the vow of chastity, which simply means abstention from the sexual relations. Just a few years ago, Pope John Paul II made it quite clear that there would be no change in this requirement any time in the near or foreseeable future.

The practice of celibacy has had a gradual development over the centuries. Even in the days of the New Testament, there was an unnatural asceticism beginning to manifest itself, which was condemned by the apostle Paul when he wrote:

> **"Celibacy" is the requirement by the Roman Catholic Church that its priests and monks do not marry.**

> Now the Spirit speaketh expressly, that in the latter times some shall depart from the faith, giving heed to seducing spirits, and doctrines of devils; speaking lies in hypocrisy; having their conscience seared with a hot iron; forbidding to marry, and commanding to abstain from meats, which God hath created to be received with thanksgiving of them which believe and know the truth (1 Tim. 4:1-3).

There were those who voluntarily gave themselves to celibacy, and that was a good and noble gesture. Jesus spoke of such in Matthew 19:12 when He said, "For there are some eunuchs, which were so born from their mother's womb: and there are some eunuchs, which were made eunuchs of men: and there be eunuchs, which have made themselves eunuchs for the kingdom of heaven's sake. He that is able to receive it, let him receive it." Celibacy itself is not wrong. But it is wrong and unnatural to demand it of an entire group of people. Paul said to forbid to marry was a doctrine of devils. The profound effect of this requirement upon those who live under it can be seen in the diminishing ranks of the Roman Catholic priesthood.

The earliest decree concerning this was issued by the Council of Elvira in A.D. 305. It said, "Let bishops, priests, and deacons, and in general all clergy who are specially employed in the service of the altar, abstain from conjugal intercourse with their wives and the begetting of children; let those who persist be degraded from the ranks of the clergy." Very little effort was made to enforce this, but it shows that even those who had moved so far from the truth in such a short time were still married men.

In the First Lateran Council of 1123, marriage in the sacred orders was said to be invalid, and finally on November 11, 1563, the Council of Trent forbade marriage to the clergy. The demand for celibacy is an arbitrary law that evolved from an unnatural asceticism that was condemned by Paul in the first place.

I know of no other group better able to tell us what effect celibacy has upon those forced to live in a celibate state than those who had lived in it. At the same time I recognize that there may be some hesitancy on the part of Roman Catholic readers to accept the statements made by former priests. I ask only that you consider what these men have to say. Personally I know of several Roman Catholic priests who left the priesthood to get married, and I imagine that there are few practicing Catholics who could not think of a few themselves. Perhaps they felt the same effects as the men who will be quoted here.

From Those Who Lived It

L.H. Lehmann, author of *The Soul of a Priest*, had this to say in his book:

The saddest experiences of my years as a priest are the evidences I found everywhere of the broken hopes and crushed ideals of priests, young and old, the same in every country that I visited. Imposed celibacy is the primary cause of the failure of which priests themselves are most fully conscious. Not that the physical implications of celibacy are a matter of great moment; it should never have been made a matter of importance. Had it not been imposed to serve the ends of papal power, but left to free, voluntary choice, priestly celibacy might have been a real service. Instead it has been made the cause of scandal and shame to the Christian church. Forced as it is by human and not divine law, it has perverted any good that otherwise might have come from it. It has had the effect of belittling the sanctity of the marriage revelation; for the only object which it can attain is the denial to priests of legal marriage rights, not abstention from sexual indulgence. The pope alone can absolve a priest who avails himself of civil sanction to contract marriage relation; private sexual aberrations can be either concealed, or absolved by recourse to an ordinary confessor.

But the real evil consequent upon forced clerical celibacy is its *enervating effect upon the bodily and mental faculties. It saps all the vigor of manhood from those who must employ the continual force of mind and will against the natural bodily urge.* Its victims have to confess that, far from freeing them from the sexual urge, it actually breeds a very ferment of impurity in the mind.

Totally at variance with that induced pious belief of the Irish about their priests, which I had shared from my youth, were my findings among them during my ministry upon three continents. Not one in a hundred was free from a tense bodily and mental struggle with the sex urge (120-124).

Let us now hear from Emmett McLoughlin, admittedly held in low esteem by Roman Catholic authorities, but one who must be recognized as a respected administrator of a major Phoenix hospital. He speaks as a former priest and is the author of *People's Padre*. From that book we read:

The life of a priest is an extremely lonely one. If he lives in a large rectory, he is still lonely. Other priests are not interested in him or in his doubts and scruples. If he is the only priest in a solitary parish or desert mission, he is still more alone.

As his years slip by and the memories of seminary and its rigidity fade away, the realization may dawn that this life is not supernatural but a complete mental and physical frustration. He sees in his parish and his community the normal life from which he has been cut off. He sees the spontaneous childhood which he was denied. He sees the innocent normal companionship of adolescence which for him never existed. He performs the rites of matrimony, as starry-eyed young men and women pledge to each other the most natural rights and pleasures. He stands alone and lonely at the altar as they turn from him and confidently, recklessly, happily step into their future home, family, work, and troubles and the successes of a normal life.

More than anything else, he seeks companionship, the companionship of normal people, not frustrated, disillusioned victims like himself. He wants the company of men and women, young and old, through whom he may at least vicariously take part in a relationship with others that has been denied him and for which, at least subconsciously, the depths of his nature craves.

The number who rebel against the frustration and unnaturalness of this form of life is far greater than anyone realizes. No one knows how many priests have quit the Roman Catholic Church in America. I know of approximately one hundred. Most ex-priests do not reveal their identity (93-94).

This was written over fifty years ago and the number of defections has increased. The Roman Catholic diocesan newspapers are crying out about the lack of priests and the lack of those who even begin the studies toward being a priest. It is reaching crisis stage, and the required celibacy plays an important part in that.

Certainly the mental and emotional distress suffered by many who are forced to live in a celibate state by required celibacy is a negative effect of this manmade law, but to my mind it is not the worst effect. Here we have a group of men who are supposed to be the spiritual leaders and guides for their people, the ones to whom their parishioners should turn in time of troubles, and they are totally unequipped to deal with one of the most important aspects of life. Their lack of preparation and understanding in this area must color their advice and reasoning in other areas as well.

Again, from *People's Padre*, McLoughlin writes:

The Roman Catholic priest is supposed to teach his parishioners how to live in marriage, when marital relations should or should not be had, how to solve the big and little problems of conjugal life. His word is final, above that of the trained counselor, the family physician, or the psychologist.

But the Roman Catholic priest can no better teach or counsel people about marriage than the paint salesman can advise the artist, or a stonecutter guide the sculptor. The blind cannot teach art. Those born deaf cannot conduct symphonies.

The Roman Catholic priest actually knows nothing about marriage except that sex is involved and lots of little Catholics are its desired result. The priest, in his thinking, contrasts celibacy with marriage. Celibacy means simply the inhibition of sex. Marriage, to him, means the satisfaction of its urge—little more.

Many things happen in marriage besides the act that leads to procreation, but the Roman Catholic priest's ignorance makes him unequipped to advise others about them. He has no concept of the softer, enduring, satisfying, non-sexual aspects of marriage, such as the intellectual compliment between two people, the emotional balancing between a man and a woman (91).

In Conclusion

There are severe problems with enforced clerical celibacy and yet the Roman Catholic authorities continue to demand it of *some* of their priests. In the final paragraph of the section dealing with celibacy in *The New Catholic Encyclopedia* we find:

> The law of celibacy is of ecclesiastical origin and may therefore be abrogated by the Church. In the early Church and in the East the marriage of bishops, priests, and deacons was permitted for good reason. In recent times, Pius XII, John XXIII, and Paul VI have found similarly good reason to dispense from celibacy in the case of married Protestant pastors who converted and desired ordination (III: 374).

Roman Catholic authorities admit that celibacy is a manmade law. That it is dispensed with at times is also admitted. Yet in spite of tremendous problems, the majority of Catholic priests are still forced to live in such an unnatural state. Why? Surely we can see that our Lord would not, and did not, demand such a thing of any of His people. It is not of Him and it is none of His. Those who seek to impose such a manmade law to the detriment of any cannot claim to be following Christ either.

"Rejoice Not In Iniquity":
Scandal in the Modern Roman Catholic Church

The Roman Catholic Church has found itself awash in a sea of scandal relating to sexual misconduct by priests. The misconduct has been primarily the abuse of young boys by homosexual pedophiles in the priesthood. The scandal involves not only the acts of abuse themselves, but the efforts of the Roman Catholic hierarchy in the United States to cover them up.

The following is a thumbnail sketch of the principle events that unfolded as this tale of sin and ungodliness came to light. The timeline, as well as the research that went into it, comes via *The Indianapolis Star*, March 24, 2002 issue of that newspaper. I use it with their permission.

On January 9, 2002, "Cardinal Law of Boston apologized for the crimes of the Reverend John J. Geoghan and implemented a zero-tolerance policy for sexual abuse by priests." On January 30, 2002, the Archdiocese of Boston turned over to the authorities the names of dozens of former priests, dating back forty years, who left the clergy because of allegations of child abuse.

Within the six days of February 2-7, 2002, "Eight active priests who were suspended from the Archdiocese of Boston admitted allegations of sexual misconduct, and at least twenty names of current and former priests were delivered to the Massachusetts district attorney. On February 9 and 10, the dioceses of Worchester, Massachusetts, and Portland, Maine, announced that they would reveal the names of priests who had histories of pedophilia, and on February 15, 2002, the diocese of Manchester, New Hampshire, said that it had given the prosecutor the names of fourteen priests who had been accused of sexually abusing children from 1963 to 1987.

On February 22, 2002, "The Archdiocese of Philadelphia revealed it had recently dismissed all remaining diocesan priests it had ever determined engaged in sexual conduct with a minor. It admitted knowing of thirty-five priests who abused about fifty children during the past fifty years." The Archdiocese of Saint Louis announced on February 26, 2002, that a priest had been removed as a fifteen-year-old sexual abuse charge against him had been revealed. Also on February 26, Cardinal Bevilacqua of Philadelphia publicly apologized to victims of sexual abuse by priests in his archdiocese and promised that no toleration of child abuse would be allowed.

On March 1, 2002, "The Archdiocese of Boston agreed to turn over the names of people allegedly molested by priests and details of the incidents." March 3 found several southern California priests told to retire or leave their ministries by Cardinal Mahony due to their part in past sexual abuse cases. On March 8, 2002, "The bishop of Palm Beach, Florida, Anthony O'Connell, resigned after admitting he sexually abused a student twenty-five years earlier, and on March 12, the church reached a settlement with eighty-six of Geoghan's alleged two hundred victims that could reach thirty million dollars."

On March 16, 2002, "Court documents revealed that New York Cardinal Egan, while bishop of the Bridgeport, Connecticut diocese, did not aggressively investigate sexual abuse allegations, did not refer complaints to criminal authorities and allowed priests to continue working for years after allegations were made." March 18 found the Archdiocese of Miami choosing not to appeal the Florida Supreme Court ruling that prohibited the use of the First Amendment to protect the Archdiocese against lawsuits alleging that sexual abuse by priests had taken place, and on March 19, "The Archdiocese of Miami confirmed that church leaders had paid several men to keep quiet about sexual abuse allegations against a priest who resigned in August, 1999."

On Friday, March 15, *The Cincinnati Enquirer* reported that as "many as five priests in the Archdiocese of Cincinnati who had been accused of sexual misconduct with teens were still serving in priestly roles." In August of 2003, the *Enquirer* quoted the Archbishop of Covington, Kentucky as saying that eight percent of the priests in his diocese had engaged in sexual misconduct over the last thirty years. Michael S. Rose, a noted Catholic editor and author of *Goodbye, Good Men*, (26), wrote, "It is a scandal of untold proportions, at least a hundred times worse than what the media have already uncovered in the United States."

Even as we recoil in horror at the revelations of such abuse, it would be a grievous error indeed to think that sexual misconduct is limited to the Roman Catholic clergy. Such is not the case. Other religious organizations have also experienced the shame of sexual sins among their leaders. Yet it must be admitted that the sexual abuse by some of the Roman Catholic clergy is astonishing due to the size of the problem and the extent to which the hierarchy went to cover it up.

I believe there are a few significant factors that have contributed to the abuse itself and to the cover-up in the Catholic Church. However, as one considers these matters, it is ungodly to make wild, salacious, and unsubstantiated accusations against the Roman Catholic Church. The sexual misconduct of some Roman Catholic priests has even become the subject of jokes. It is not funny, and true children of God do not delight in the iniquity of anyone.

The sexual misconduct of some Roman Catholic priests has even become the subject of jokes. It is not funny, and true children of God do not delight in the iniquity of anyone.

There is a view being widely expressed now in the wake of the revelations of priestly sexual misconduct that forced celibacy among the Roman Catholic clergy is to blame. While I do believe that it may be a contributing factor, I also feel that forced celibacy is within itself the result of a much deeper problem. The Roman Catholic Church has traditionally held an unhealthy and decidedly non-biblical view of sex.

Early in the development of Mariology that is so peculiarly Catholic, a less than healthy and certainly unbiblical view of physical relations between a man and a woman began to surface. Instead of just accepting the fact that Jesus was born of a virgin in fulfillment of prophecy, uninspired men felt compelled to offer their own explanations. As early as A.D. 390, we find the synod at Milan condemning the proposition that "a virgin conceived, but a virgin did not bring forth." What the council condemned was simply the idea that during the natural course of the birth, Mary's hymen was broken and the passage opened. In his famous work, *Sermons*, Augustine wrote, "For as a virgin she conceived, as a virgin she gave birth, a virgin she remained" (51). In *De Trinitate* he wrote, "For neither do we know the countenance of the Virgin

Mary, from whom, untouched by a husband, nor tainted in the birth itself, He was wonderfully born" (8,5).

The idea that normal physical relations between a husband and a wife somehow "taint" the woman is found as early as the fourth century. Siricius, who lived from A.D 334-399, called a "saint" by the Catholic Church, and claimed as one of their popes, wrote the following in a letter, cited in *Twenty-Five Questions Non-Catholics Ask*:

> We surely cannot deny that you were right in correcting the doctrines about children of Mary, and Your Holiness was right in rejecting the idea that any other offspring should come from the same virginal womb from which Christ was born according to the flesh. For the Lord Jesus would not have chosen to be born of a virgin if he had judged that she would be so incontinent as to taint the birthplace of the body of the Lord, the home of the eternal king, with the seed of human intercourse (87).

Bible students know that the relationship between a husband and wife is so holy and good that Paul compared it to the relationship sustained between Christ and His church in Ephesians 5. Bible students also recognize that the Hebrew letter states, "Let marriage be held in honor among all, and let the marriage bed be undefiled" (Heb. 13:4). There is nothing incontinent, unholy, or tainted in any way in the normal physical relations between a husband and wife.

I mention this because I believe it shows the early seeds of an unbiblical view of the gift of sex, and begins to lay the foundation of the attitude that has given rise to the sexual abuse that is rampant in the Roman Catholic Church today.

What about celibacy? The forced celibacy of the Catholic clergy is receiving a lot of attention in view of the revelations of sexual misconduct. But why has celibacy been enjoined upon the Roman Catholic clergy in the first place? The Roman Catholic Church has traditionally held that celibacy is inherently better, that it is a holier state. In *The Catholic Encyclopedia* we find:

> Although we do not find in the New Testament any indication of celibacy being made compulsory either upon the Apostles or those whom they ordained, we have ample warrant in the language of Our Savior, and of St. Paul for looking upon virginity as the higher call, and by inference, as the condition befitting those who are set apart for the work of the ministry (III: 481).

The encyclopedia makes reference to Paul's words in 1 Corinthians 7:7, "Yet I wish that all men were even as I myself am" and makes no mention of how the "present distress" of verse 26 colors the words of the Holy Spirit. One paragraph later the encyclopedia states:

> From the earliest period the Church was personified and conceived of by her disciples as the Virgin Bride and as the pure Body of Christ, or again as the Virgin Mother, and it was plainly fitting that this virgin Church should be served by a virgin priesthood. . . .The conviction that virginity possesses a higher sanctity and clearer spiritual intuitions, seems to be an instinct planted deep in the heart of man (III: 481).

This concept of no sexual activity being a state that is somehow purer, holier, and more righteous gave rise to the unnatural and unbiblical practice of forced celibacy. It is unnatural because God said, "It is not good for man to be alone" (Gen. 2:18), and "But because of immoralities, let each man have his own wife, and let each woman have her own husband" (1 Cor. 7:2). To demand celibacy is unbiblical because the Holy Spirit declared through Paul, in 1 Timothy 4:1-3, that to do such was to pay "attention to deceitful spirits and doctrines of demons." Voluntary celibacy is not wrong. But it is wrong and sinful, as well as unnatural, to demand it.

Voluntary celibacy is not wrong. But it is wrong and sinful, as well as unnatural, to demand it.

Beginning with the development of the hermitic lifestyle in the second and third centuries, and the view of some that such a lifestyle produced the highest form of spiritual piety, we find that, as people moved further away from the simple truths of God's word and the Roman Catholic denomination began to develop, there was a movement to impose this lifestyle on all members of its clergy. Various councils through the centuries issued decrees concerning it, some as early as A.D. 305. The Council of Trent in 1563 decreed, "Whoever shall affirm that the conjugal state is to be preferred to a life of virginity or celibacy, and that it is not better and more conducive to happiness to remain in virginity or celibacy, than to be married, let him be accursed."

Today, the *Code of Canon Law, Latin-English Edition* (1983, Canon 277) states:

> Clerics are obliged to observe perfect and perpetual continence for the sake of the kingdom of heaven and therefore are obliged to observe celibacy, which is a special gift of God, by which sacred ministers can adhere more easily to Christ

with an undivided heart and can more freely dedicate themselves to the service of God and humankind.

It is obvious that this state of forced celibacy, brought about by the Roman Catholic view of virginity as being holier and purer than the marriage bed, is having a tremendously detrimental and dangerous effect upon many living under it. This, as well as a preoccupation with sexual sins and conduct in Roman Catholicism, contributes to a decidedly unhealthy view of sex and its righteous practice among many of the Roman Catholic clergy.

The men who comprise the Roman Catholic priesthood, deprived of the God-given outlet for sexual feelings, as well as the wonderful blessings of the companionship in all other ways of a wife, are still supposed to act as spiritual counselors to those who have experienced marriage. They are to be confessors to whom their parishioners confess their deepest thoughts and sins of a sexual nature. It is a major part of life that they have been denied. How are they prepared to deal with such problems?

Let's move on to the second and final thing that I would like to discuss. What takes this story from the realm of disturbing and tragic to scandalous is the fact that the Roman Catholic Church has been hiding such activity for years and has failed to abide by the laws of this country pertaining to such criminal acts. The priests who committed these acts are criminals and should have been treated as such by the hierarchy of the Roman Catholic Church— not sent for a few months of treatment and then reassigned to other parishes. The Roman Catholic hierarchy has failed in their responsibility to abide by the laws of this country.

It is my conviction that the flaunting of the laws of this country by the hierarchy is a natural consequence of the Roman Catholic belief that their church is above all human government and answerable to no one on earth. I recognize that in the lives of those who are truly Christians the first obligation is to God. If the government under which we live should seek to require us to violate a precept of God, then, as Peter said, "We must obey God rather than men" (Acts 5:29). At the same time I also recognize the Christian's responsibility to be subject to the government under which we live. Paul makes that abundantly clear in Romans 13:1-6.

If ever there was a case of the laws of the government being designed to protect its people, it would be the laws against pedophilia. There can be no justifiable explanation for the actions of the Roman Catholic hierarchy concerning sexual abuse of children by its priests. However, the fact that there is no justifiable explanation does not mean that there is no explanation at all.

Within Roman Catholicism there are what are called Ecclesiastical Privileges. According to the *Catholic Encyclopedia*, these "are exceptions to the law made in favor of the clergy or in favor of consecrated and sacred objects or places." One of these privileges is known as "Privigelium Fori." This is the way the *Catholic Encyclopedia* describes it:

> This secures the clergy a special tribunal in civil and criminal causes before an ecclesiastical judge. The civil causes of clerics pertain by nature to the secular courts as much as those of the laity. But the thought that it was unseemly that the fathers and teachers of the faithful should be brought before laymen as judges, and also the experience that many laymen were greatly inclined to oppress the clergy, led the Church to withdraw her servants even in civil matters from the secular courts, and to bring them entirely under her own jurisdiction. . . . From early times, however, it met with great opposition from the State. With the growing ascendancy of the State over the Church, the privilege was more and more limited, and was finally everywhere abrogated.

> Today, according to secular law, the civil and criminal causes of clerics belong to the lay court. Only with respect to the purely spiritual conditions of their station and office, are clerics subject to their bishop, and then not without certain state limitations—especially with respect to certain practical punishments. *However, the church maintains in principle the privilegium fori.*

I believe that the actions of the Roman Catholic hierarchy related to the cover-up of the abuse of children by priests for years is a direct result of the attitude displayed by this "privilege." The Roman Catholic Church believes that it is the supreme authority on earth, ecclesiastical or civil. It does not believe in the separation of church and state and claims that it has the final voice of authority. Ultimately it doesn't matter what is "according to secular law," if that does not serve the best interest of the Roman Catholic Church.

In 1864 Pope Pius IX issued what has come to be known as *The Syllabus of Errors*. Its official title is "A syllabus containing the most important errors of our time which have been condemned by our Holy Father Pius IX in allocutions, at consistories, in encyclicals and other apostolic letters." There are eighty so-called "errors" set forth in the Syllabus. I want to give you just a few, and I am presenting them in their positive form. In other words, it is not necessary to add anything to them to understand their meanings:

#42 – In legal conflict between Powers (Civil and Ecclesiastical), the Ecclesiastical Law prevails.

#54 – Kings and Princes (including, of course, Presidents, Prime Ministers, etc.) are not only not exempt from the jurisdiction of the Church, but are subordinate to the Church in litigated questions of jurisdiction.

#55 – The Church ought to be in union with the State, and the State with the Church.

#57 – Philosophical principles, moral science, and civil laws may and must be made to bend to Divine and Ecclesiastical authority.

In the *Catholic Encyclopedia* we read, "For the Syllabus, as appears from the official communication of Cardinal Antonelli, is a decision given by the pope speaking as universal teacher and judge to Catholics the world over. All Catholics, therefore, are bound to accept the Syllabus" (368-369).

It is undeniable that the Roman Catholic hierarchy considers the Church to be above civil law, and ultimately, not answerable to it. It is my firm conviction that the cases of sexual abuse of children by priests were not reported to proper civil authorities because to do so was determined by members of the Roman Catholic hierarchy not to be in the Church's best interest. In their teaching, the interest of the Church must always take precedence. The atmosphere of superiority allows them to believe that they are above the law, even the criminal laws designed to protect the citizens of our nation, or any other nation.

The Mass

In the New Testament we find first century Christians engaging in simple worship that consisted of five different acts. These acts were partaking of the Lord's Supper, vocal singing, giving of their means, study or preaching, and prayer. The acts of partaking of the Lord's Supper and giving of their means were peculiar to the first day of the week, Sunday. This is how Christians were taught to worship by the apostles and other inspired men, and this is what they did.

Historically we can see that this was a pattern that continued for some time. From the pen of Justin Martyr, a second-century apologist, we are given a full account of a second-century worship service in his *Apology*. He wrote:

> And on the day called Sunday there is a gathering together in the same place of all who live in a city or a rural district. The memoirs of the apostles or the writings of the prophets are read, as long as time permits. Then when the reader ceases, the president in a discourse admonishes and urges the imitation of these good things. Next we all rise together and send up prayers. And, as I said before, when we cease from our prayer, bread is presented and wine and water. The president in the same manner sends up prayers and thanksgivings according to his ability, and the people sing out their assent saying the "Amen." A distribution and participation of the elements for which thanks have been given is made to each person, and to those who are not present it is sent by the deacons. Those who have means and are willing, each according to his own choice, gives what he wills, and what is collected is deposited with the president (I: 67).

This then gives us proof that at least for 125 years or so, the church conformed to the simple New Testament pattern of worship given by the Lord Jesus through the Holy Spirit. The Lord's Church today continues to worship according to this simple, God-given pattern.

However, in Roman Catholic churches throughout the world something very different has been substituted for worship. It is called the "Mass."

The Nature of the Mass

The Mass is the supreme act of worship according to Catholic teaching and thus any study of Catholicism necessarily must address itself to an understanding of this belief and practice. The first question that needs to be answered is, "What is the Mass?"

According to *The Question Box* by Conway, in Canons 1-5 the Council of Trent thus declared the Catholic Church's teaching concerning the Mass:

1. There is in the Catholic Church *a true sacrifice, the Mass,* instituted by Jesus Christ—*the Sacrifice of His Body and Blood under the appearances of bread and wine.*

2. *This Sacrifice is identical with the Sacrifice of the Cross,* inasmuch as Jesus Christ is Priest and Victim in both; *the only difference lies in the manner of offering,* which is bloody upon the Cross and bloodless on our altars.

3. It is propitiatory Sacrifice, atoning for our sins, and the sins of the living and of the dead in Christ, for whom it is offered.

4. Its efficacy is derived from the Sacrifice of the Cross, whose infinite merits it applies to us.

5. Although offered to God alone, it may be celebrated in honor and memory of the saints.

6. The Mass was instituted at the Last Supper when Christ, about to offer Himself on the altar of the Cross by His death (Heb. xi. 5) for our redemption (Heb. ix. 12), wished to endow His Church with a *visible Sacrifice,* commemorative of His Bloody Sacrifice of the Cross. As High Priest, according to the order of Melchisedech (Ps. cix. 9), He offered to His Father His own Body and Blood under the appearances of bread and wine, and constituted His Apostles priests of the New Testament to renew this same offering until He came again (1 Cor. xi. 26) by the words, "Do this in commemoration of Me" (Luke xxii. 19; 1 Cor. xi. 34).

So in the simplest terms, we can say that the Roman Catholic Mass is taught to be a sacrifice, identical with the offering of our Lord upon the Cross of Calvary.

Emmett McLoughlin, a former Franciscan priest, had this to say in his book, *American Culture & Catholic Schools:*

The oldest and greatest religious political system, the Roman Catholic hierarchy, has made the fullest possible use of man's emotional need for rituals. It has supplied them for all ages, all moods, and all occasions. The most important of these is the Mass. The Roman Church has, over the centuries, taken the simple farewell gathering of the last supper and, with a kaleidoscope of color, an oriental ornateness of sacred vessels, and an overwhelming richness of symbolism, built up a liturgical ritualism that overwhelms the senses, especially of the young (67).

Even *The New Catholic Encyclopedia* admits, "The Mass of today differs greatly from the very simple ceremony followed by Christ and His apostles" (419). Such a statement lends itself to a question and a conclusion. Since the Roman Catholic Mass differs greatly from what Christ and His apostles did, where did it come from? How did it come to be? Additionally, since it does differ so dramatically from the practice of the first century church, we are going to be examining a manmade practice, not something taught by Christ or His inspired apostles.

The Development of the Mass

The name, "Mass," comes from the Latin word *Missa*, which means "dismissal." A practice that evolved prohibited those who were not yet Christians from remaining in the worship service while the Lord's Supper was being observed. After scripture reading and teaching, they were dismissed while the Christians remained. Hence, the use of the word *Missa*. The first to use the term to describe the whole of the worship service were Gregory of Tours and Gregory the Great, both of the sixth century.

Until Vatican II, the Roman Catholic Mass was said in Latin; now it is generally said in the language of the people where the Mass is taking place. The original language was Greek. It was superceded by Latin early in the fifth century.

We can find significant and noticeable changes from the simple worship service of the first century beginning to surface in the third century, 250 years after the establishment of the church. Man was beginning to introduce his own ideas into what God had specified. Instead of all Christians sharing equally in worship to the Lord, a separate class began to develop of individuals who assumed unauthorized positions of prominence in the worship services. As time went on and individuals felt free to abandon or add to God's revealed way, a great variety of worship services began to appear. This variety presented the need for some sort of uniformity of worship, so Gregory the Great (590-604) sought reforms to simplify worship and make it uniform throughout those churches over which he exercised authority. It is interesting that the liturgy of the Roman Church Latin worship can be found no earlier than the sixth century. However, Gregory's reforms did not prove to be normative throughout the Roman Church.

As we move into the eighth century, we find a desire among European, particularly Frankish, kings for uniformity of worship in their realms. From *Doors to the Sacred*, by Joseph Martos, we find, "As early as 754, Pepin, king of the Franks and Charlemagne's father, had tried to make the liturgy of Rome obligatory in his kingdom, but it was only under Charlemagne himself that the royal insistence on the more uniform liturgy in the Frankish empire began to be taken seriously." Charlemagne appointed his chancellor to adapt Gregory's liturgy, the liturgy of Rome, to the needs of the "priests" in his kingdom and decreed in 784 that the result was to be used throughout his realm.

Charlemagne's actions set in motion a process that would continue through the eleventh century. The old "Roman Liturgy" began to take on a decidedly Frankish flavor. It became more dramatic, more ritualistic. The common people of the church were removed further and further from the actual worship itself. Prayers became private devotions for the priests, whispered by them. The language was not the language of the people; they could not understand what was being said. Under Gregory VII all the liturgical texts were gathered together in one Roman Missal and uniformity with this more dramatic Mass was achieved for Roman Catholicism.

This did not stop additional changes. In the twelfth and thirteenth centuries the altar was turned away from the people, and the priest no longer faced the members, thus removing the common member even further from active participation. Ornamental backdrops were added, increasing the dramatic effect. Candles on the altar became customary, and more and more the Mass became the action of the priest, while the members were little more than quiet spectators.

The Roman Catholic Mass came under tremendous attack during the Protestant Reformation, both from a theological and a ceremonial standpoint. However, here we are more concerned with the ceremonial. In answer to the attacks, the Council of Trent issued these statements on September 17, 1562:

> If any one saith that the canon of the mass contains errors and is therefore to be abrogated; let him be anathema (Canon 6).

> If any one saith that the ceremonies, vestments, and outward signs, which the Catholic Church makes use of in the celebration of masses, are incentives to impiety rather than offices of piety; let him be anathema (Canon 7).

> If any one saith that the rite of the Roman Church, according to which a part of the canon and the words of the consecration are pronounced in a low tone, is to be condemned; or that the mass ought to be celebrated in the vulgar tongue only; or that water ought not to be mixed with the wine that is to be offered in the chalice, since it is contrary to the institution of Christ; let him be anathema (Canon 9).

In 1570 a normative Roman Missal was issued under the authority of Pius V and made mandatory for all of Catholicism. In 1588 Sixtus V established the Congregation of Rites to oversee all liturgical functions. Any change in the Mass from this point on had to come from the highest ecclesiastical authority. The Roman Catholic Mass said in 1960, prior to Vatican II, was practically identical, word for word and gesture for gesture, with the Roman Catholic Mass of 1570. Vatican II would take steps to bring the people more into the celebration of the Mass. Common language would be allowed, the altar would be turned around so the priest could face the people, and there would be more responses for the people to make. Other changes would take place, but the substance of the Roman Catholic Mass remains.

The Result

The Roman Catholic Mass today is a manmade, elaborate ritual that bears little or no resemblance to the simple worship authorized by Christ and practiced by the first century church. It is a drama with the priest the primary actor. Notice this statement from *Roman Catholicism* by Loraine Boettner:

> The elaborate ritual of the mass is really an extended pageant, designed to re-enact the experiences of Christ from the supper in the upper room, through the agony in the garden, the betrayal, trial, crucifixion, death, burial, resurrection, and ascension. It is a drama crowding the detailed events of many days into the space of one hour or less. For its proper performance the priest in seminary goes through long periods of training and needs a marvelous memory. Witness the following: he makes the sign of the cross sixteen times; lifts his

eyes to heaven eleven times; kisses the altar eight times; folds his hands four times; strikes his breast ten times; bows his head twenty-one times; genuflects eight times; bows his shoulders seven times; blesses the altar with the sign of the cross thirty times; lays his hands flat on the altar twenty-nine times; prays secretly eleven times; prays aloud thirteen times; take the bread and wine and turns it into the body and blood of Christ; covers and uncovers the chalice ten times; goes to and fro twenty times; and in addition performs numerous other acts (170-171).

We haven't even mentioned Roman Catholic requirements concerning the chalice, the makeup of the candles, the vestments worn, and the prayers said. The Roman Catholic Mass is a classic example of what happens when men allow their imaginations to run wild and abandon God's simple revelation. I cannot say it any better than the Roman Catholic writers themselves in *The New Catholic Encyclopedia*, "The Mass of today differs greatly from the very simple ceremony followed by Christ and His Apostles."

The apostle Paul wrote, "Those things, which ye have both learned, and received, and heard, and seen in me, do: and the God of Peace shall be with you" (Phil. 4:9). Paul neither learned, received, heard, or saw anything like the Roman Catholic Mass.

A Propitiatory Sacrifice?

In describing the Mass as the very center of Roman Catholicism, Cardinal Newman aptly stated it in *Loss and Gain*, when he wrote, "It is not a mere form of words, it is a great action, the greatest action that can be on earth. The Council of Trent declared of the Mass, 'It is a propitiatory Sacrifice, atoning for our sins, and the sins of the living and of the dead in Christ, for whom it is offered'" (XXII, chs. 1-3, Canon 3).

In each sacrifice there is the "immolation" (the killing of the sacrificial victim) and the "oblation" (the offering of that which has been killed). According to Catholic teaching the immolation of Christ occurred once and for all on the cross of Calvary. It does not need to be repeated and cannot be repeated. But the oblation, or the offering of the sacrifice that has been slain, can and must be repeated each time the Mass is offered. Christ died but once; it is the slain victim who is being offered. The Mass then is a propitiatory sacrifice, atoning for the sins of mankind every time it is offered.

Perhaps it would be better to allow Roman Catholic writers to describe it for us. In *Twenty-Five Questions Non-Catholics Ask*, Rev. John A. O'Brien writes:

The Mass is the *renewal* and perpetuation of the sacrifice of the Cross in the sense that it offers anew to God the Victim of Calvary. It thus commemorates the sacrifice of the Cross, re-enacts it symbolically and mystically, and applies the fruits of Christ's death upon the Cross to individual human souls. All the efficacy of the Mass is derived therefore from the sacrifice of Calvary.

The sacrifice of the Mass is offered up for the same ends for which Christ died on the Cross, namely, *to propitiate Almighty God for the sins of man,* to render homage, praise and thanksgiving for His benefits, and to supplicate Him for graces and blessings (64-65).

The Mass is the renewal and perpetuation of the sacrifice of the Cross in the sense that it offers anew to God the Victim of Calvary.

Such teaching leads one to question, "How can Christ, who suffered, died, arose from the grave, and ascended into glory with the Father, possibly be offered time and time again as that which is slain?" The Roman Catholic answer to that is found in *The Question Box*: "The Church has never defined in what manner Christ is a Victim in the Mass, *but has left this question to the speculations of the theologians*" (264). The theologians of the Catholic Church did speculate, and the results of their speculations have been many and varied. But what is apparently the most widely held view is presented in *The Last Supper and Calvary* by Maurice de la Taille:

> The Mass is a Sacrifice and a true Sacrifice, insofar as, by means of a symbolic immolation, it is a true and actual oblation of a true Victim, although it contains no real immolation of Christ actually performed by us, but only a symbolic one, coupled with that state of Victim, perennial and celestial, due to the one real and bloody immolation undergone by Christ in days gone by. The Mass is a Sacrifice, because it is our oblation of the Victim once immolated, even as the Supper was the oblation of the Victim to be immolated.

This then is the nature of the Roman Catholic Mass. It is the continuation of the sacrifice of Calvary. It is the unbloody offering, the oblation, of the once-slain or immolated Christ. It is a propitiatory, or atoning, sacrifice, instituted at the Last Supper as Jesus wished to endow His church with a *visible sacrifice. The New Code of Canon Law*, 1983, says of it:

> The celebration of the Eucharist is the action of Christ Himself and the Church; in it Christ the Lord, by the ministry of a priest, *offers Himself, substantially*

present under the forms of bread and wine, to God the Father and gives Himself as spiritual food to the faithful who are associated with His offering (889).

Of God or Of Man?

Is the Mass a continuation of the sacrifice of Calvary? Is it the repeated oblation of the victim once immolated? Is it truly Christ offering Himself, by the ministry of the priest, hundreds of times a day across the globe?

Great pains are taken by Roman Catholic authorities to make the point that the death of Jesus on the cross is not being repeated in the Mass, but merely continued. Hundreds of times a day on Roman Catholic altars across the globe, a propitiatory sacrifice, one that atones for sins, is said to be made. It is not the immolation of the actual Victim, but the oblation, or the offering of Him, in an unbloody fashion. Every day Jesus Christ is really, truly, and substantially offered on altars in sacrifice through the ministry of Roman Catholic priests. But is this true, according to the teaching of the New Testament? Is it necessary to make an offering for sin daily—actually hundreds of times a day—or is this another example of the imaginations of Catholic theologians running wild?

In Hebrews 7:26-27 we find, "For such an high priest became us, who is holy, harmless, undefiled, separate from sinners, and made higher than the heavens; Who needeth not daily, as those high priests, to offer up sacrifices, first for his own sins, and then for the people's: for this he did once, when he offered up himself." Notice the word, "once," in verse 27. That word is *hapax*, and it means "once, without need or possibility of repetition; finally." We find the same word used several times in Hebrews 9:22-28:

> And almost all things are by the law purged with blood: and without shedding of blood is no remission. It was therefore necessary that the patterns of things in the heavens should be purified with these; but the heavenly things themselves with better sacrifices than these. For Christ is not entered in to the holy places made with hands, which are the figures of the true; but into heaven itself, now to appear in the presence of God for us: *nor yet that he should offer himself often*, as the high priest entereth into the holy place every year with blood of others; for then must he often have suffered since the foundation of the world: but now *once* in the end of the world hath he appeared to put away sin by the sacrifice of himself. And as it is appointed unto man *once* to die, but after this the judgment; so Christ was *once* offered to bear the sins of many.

Each time it is used it means the same thing—"once, without need or possibility of repetition; finally." So if Jesus Christ is offered repeatedly on a daily basis on Roman Catholic altars across the world, does that also mean that He has appeared on this earth repeatedly, over and over and over again? Does it mean that people, you and I, can die repeatedly? Does it mean that we are going to have several chances as far as judgment is concerned? No, it does not; and Jesus Christ is not offered repeatedly, over and over and over again, on Catholic altars either.

Whatever the Roman Catholic Mass is, it is not the continuation of Jesus' sacrifice on Calvary; it is not a propitiatory sacrifice atoning for sins. God's Word tells us that that happened only once, that Christ does not offer Himself often (as Catholic doctrine teaches) and that when Jesus shed His blood on Calvary it was to put away sin. Jesus was *once offered to bear the sins of many.*

If there could still be any question, Hebrews 10:12-18 tells us:

Whatever the Roman Catholic Mass is, it is not the continuation of Jesus' sacrifice on Calvary; it is not a propitiatory sacrifice atoning for sins.

But this man, after he had offered one sacrifice for sins forever, sat down on the right hand of God; from henceforth expecting till his enemies be made his footstool. For by one offering he hath perfected forever them that are sanctified. Whereof the Holy Ghost also is a witness to us: for after that he had said before, This is the covenant that I will make with them after those days, saith the Lord, I will put my laws into their hearts, and in their minds will I write them; and their sins and iniquities will I remember no more. *Now where remission of these is, there is no more offering for sins.*

If in fact the sacrifice of Jesus on the cross was successful, if in fact it was for the remission of sins and sins were remitted and are remitted through that offering, then according to God's Word "there is no more offering for sin." The Mass cannot be a "renewal" of the sacrifice of the Cross, it cannot "offer *anew* to God the Victim of Calvary." To say that it does and must is to say that Christ failed on the cross.

Roman Catholic teaching tells us that Christ instituted the Mass at the Last Supper, wishing to endow His church with a "visible sacrifice." This would necessitate Jesus having offered Himself at the Last Supper, before the crucifixion. If the Mass is an *actual* sacrifice instituted at the Last Supper, then the Last Supper had to be an *actual sacrifice* as well. How could it possibly have been the *identical* sacrifice as Calvary when that sacrifice had not yet taken place? How could it have been the *continuation* of that sacrifice when as yet that sacrifice had not been offered? The answer to both questions is that it couldn't.

The amazing thing to me is that Catholic doctrine concerning the Mass being a propitiatory sacrifice contradicts the wording of one of their own authorized versions of the Bible. This is how the *Good News Bible* (Today's English Version) renders Hebrews 10:11-18:

> Every Jewish priest performs his services every day and offers the same sacrifices many times; but these sacrifices can never take away sins. Christ, however, *offered one sacrifice for sins, an offering that is effective forever,* and then he sat down at the right side of God. There he now awaits until God puts his enemies as a footstool under his feet. With one sacrifice, then, he has made perfect forever those who are purified from sin. And the Holy Spirit also gives us his witness. First he says, This is the covenant that I will make with them in the days to come, says the Lord: I will put my laws in their hearts and write them on their minds. And then he says, I will not remember their sins and evil deeds any longer. *So when these have been forgiven, an offering to take away sins is no longer needed.*

As I consider the Catholic teaching concerning the propitiatory nature of the Mass, I am reminded again of the words of our Lord, "But in vain they do worship me, teaching for doctrines the commandments of men" (Matt. 15:9).

Transubstantiation

Thinking back to my years as a parochial school student at St. John's the Evangelist in Cincinnati, Ohio, I remember well daily attendance at eight o'clock Mass. Of all the parts of the Mass, there was one that was the most exciting and spiritually uplifting, one that never became boring or commonplace. That time was during the Canon of the Mass when the consecration took place. To the accompaniment of tinkling altar bells, the priest would take the wafer of unleavened bread (the host), hold it between the thumb and the first two fingers of his hands, lift it up toward heaven, and proclaim, "This is my body." Then he would take the chalice, the cup lined with gold and filled with sacramental wine mingled with water, raise it toward heaven, and proclaim, "This is my blood." With his words and the tinkling of the bells being the only sounds in an otherwise silent church building, and with all eyes fastened upon the host or the chalice, it was a most moving time.

Transubstantiation is the name given to the change that is believed by Roman Catholics to take place in the sacrament of the Holy Eucharist.

At first I did not know the significance of what was taking place, but being a young child, the drama of the moment was enough. Later, as the years went by and I reached the higher grades of elementary school, I came to learn the specifics of the act. I came to learn what was really supposed to be taking place and the name of it. The specific belief that was the most awe-inspiring was called "transubstantiation."

What Is Transubstantiation?

Transubstantiation is the name given to the change that is believed by Roman Catholics to take place in the sacrament of the Holy Eucharist. According to *The Catechism of the Catholic Church* this sacrament is called several different names, such as the Lord's Supper, the Breaking of Bread, the Eucharistic Assembly, the Memorial of the Lord's Passion and Resurrection, the Holy Sacrifice, the Holy and Divine Liturgy, and the Most Blessed Sacrament, among others (335-336). Each name is said to evoke certain aspects of the sacrament.

As far as the specific doctrine of transubstantiation is concerned, *The Catechism of the Catholic Church* tells us:

> The mode of Christ's presence under the Eucharistic species is unique. It raises the Eucharist above all the sacraments as "the perfection of the spiritual life and the end to which all sacraments tend." In the most blessed sacrament of the Eucharist "the body and blood, together with the soul and divinity of our Lord Jesus Christ and, therefore, the whole Christ, is truly, really, and substantially contained." This presence is called "real" because it is present in the fullest sense: that is to say, it is a substantial presence by which Christ, God, and man, makes himself wholly and entirely present (346).

The Baltimore Catechism says, "We use the words, really, truly, and substantially, to describe Christ's presence in the Holy Eucharist in order to distinguish Our Lord's teaching from that of mere men who falsely teach that the Holy Eucharist is only a sign or a figure of Christ, or that He is present only by His power."

Again from *The Baltimore Catechism*:

> When our Lord said, "This is my body," the entire substance of the bread was changed into His body. Christ could not have used clearer, more explicit words than "This is my body." He did not say, "This is a sign of my body," or "This represents my body," but "This is my body." Catholics take Christ at His Word because He is the omnipotent God. On His Word they know that the Holy Eucharist is the body and blood of Christ (276).

In answer to the question, "Did anything of the bread and wine remain after their substance had been changed into Our Lord's body and blood?" *The Baltimore Catechism* says:

> After the substance of the bread and wine had been changed into Our Lord's body and blood, there remained only the appearances of bread and wine. Because the appearances of bread and wine remain in the Holy Eucharist, we cannot see Christ with our bodily eyes in this sacrament. We do see Him, however,

with the eyes of faith. Our bodily eyes, moreover, do not deceive us when they see the appearances of bread and wine, for these appearances really remain after the Consecration of the Mass (277).

The change of the entire substance of the bread and wine into the body and blood of Jesus is called transubstantiation. Before moving on, let's look at one more quote from *The Baltimore Catechism*. In answer to the question, "How was Our Lord able to change bread and wine into His body and blood?" we find:

> Our Lord was able to change bread and wine into His body and blood by His almighty power. God, who created all things from nothing, who fed the five thousand with five loaves, who changed water into wine instantaneously, who raised the dead to life, can change bread and wine into the body and blood of Christ. Although the Holy Eucharist is a great mystery, and consequently beyond human understanding, the principles of sound reason can show that this great gift is not impossible by the power of God (279).

So then transubstantiation is that process whereby the bread and wine of the Eucharistic Sacrifice are changed into the real body and blood of Christ. It takes place at the consecration or the Mass with the words, "This is my body" and "This is my blood" being spoken by the priest. When this change takes place, there is no physical evidence whatsoever since the bread and wine retain their color, taste, weight, shape, and everything else that appears to the senses. We have seen that this is a great mystery and consequently beyond human understanding, yet visible through the eyes of faith. Transubstantiation is one of the most integral parts of Roman Catholicism. Indeed, *The Catechism of the Catholic Church* says, "In brief, the Eucharist is the sum and summary of our faith. Our way of thinking is attended to the Eucharist and the Eucharist in turn confirms our way of thinking." To be a Roman Catholic, one must believe in the doctrine of transubstantiation. And at one point in my life, I certainly did.

Unanswered Questions

Since it is a principle of Roman Catholicism, as stated in John L. McKenzie's book, *The Roman Catholic Church,* that "No proposition can be declared an article of faith unless *perpetual belief* in the church can be affirmed of it" (212), and since *The Baltimore Catechism* stated that the Lord instituted the Holy Eucharist at the Last Supper, it stands to reason that the early church must have both believed and practiced transubstantiation. The Council of Trent, on October 11, 1551, declared:

Because Christ our Redeemer said that it was truly His body that He was offering under the species of bread, it has always been the conviction of the Church of God, and this holy Council now declares again, that by the consecration of the bread and wine there takes place a change of the whole substance of the bread into the substance of the body of Christ our Lord and of the whole substance of wine into the substance of His blood. This change the Holy Catholic Church has fittingly and properly called Transubstantiation.

Now with this being true, and it must be or transubstantiation cannot be an article of faith, why is it that we do not find any inkling of this belief until the writings of Cyril of Jerusalem in the fourth century? And why is it that in *The Book of Catholic Quotations*, bearing the Imprimatur of Francis Cardinal Spellman, we find under the heading of "The Eucharist: Sacrifice," this quoted from Justin Marty's *Dialogue with Trypho*, written in the second century:

It is quite evident that this prophecy (Isaiah 33, 13-19) also alludes to the bread which our Christ gave us to offer *in remembrance* of the Body which He assumed for the sake of those who believe in Him, for whom He also suffered, and also to the cup which He taught us to offer in the Eucharist, *in commemoration* of His Blood.

Why did Clement of Alexandria, a writer from the latter part of the second century, called by the *Catholic Encyclopedia* a "convert to the faith," write of the bread and wine in this way, "brought this out by symbols" and "describing distinctly by metaphor"?

Why is it that it was not until the Fourth Lateran Council in A.D. 1215 that transubstantiation was declared to be an article of faith? Why is that the Council of Trent saw fit to restate the doctrine on October 11, 1551?

It is obvious that the early church, under the direction of the apostles and those who lived very near the time of the apostles, did not believe in or practice transubstantiation. It is clear from their own quotations that in the second century the bread was viewed as a remembrance of the body of Christ, and not the body itself. It is equally clear that the wine was viewed as commemorating the blood of Christ and not as the blood itself. Truly, it was almost 1200 years after the establishment of the church before transubstantiation was definitively set forth as an article of faith. Doesn't it seem unlikely that all of those infallible popes over that 1200-year period did not see fit to declare transubstantiation an article of faith if they themselves believed and practiced it? The statement from *The Catechism of the Catholic Church* that it "has always been the conviction of the Church of God" is just not true.

As we earlier noted, *The Baltimore Catechism* attempts to prove transubstantiation by calling upon God's power and ability to do such a thing. Now I certainly do not doubt the power of God, but I do doubt the logic of the reasoning of the Catholic authorities. The miracles that they used to prove their point (creating all things from nothing, feeding the five thousand with five loaves, changing water into wine instantaneously, and raising the dead to life) prove far too much. In each case there was substantial evidence that a miracle had taken place. When God created all things from nothing, where there had been nothing there was then all things—real things that could be seen and touched. When five thousand were fed with five loaves, five thousand ate something that was real, that could be chewed and tasted. When they were filled, there was much evidence of the miracle left over. When the water was changed into wine, it did not retain the physical qualities of water; it became wine. When Lazarus was raised from the dead, Lazarus himself was evidence of the miracle. The point is that the miracles were faith-producing, not faith-dependent. When our Lord performed a miracle, there was ample evidence that a miracle had taken place. The evidence of transubstantiation is that nothing has happened. An appeal to faith is not sufficient. God's miracles *produced* faith; they did not *depend* on it.

> **The evidence of transubstantiation is that nothing has happened. An appeal to faith is not sufficient. God's miracles *produced* faith; they did not *depend* on it.**

As far as the Scriptures are concerned, Roman Catholic authorities expressed the sentiment that they were on very solid ground in their belief, taking Jesus at His word as opposed to those who do not. That in itself is very interesting, for that same Jesus said in Matthew 23:9-10, "And call no man your father upon the earth: for one is your Father, which is in heaven. Neither be ye called masters: for one is your Master, even Christ." In this passage our Lord forbade the use of titles in religion to elevate one man above another. Every priest I know goes by the title, "Father." So much for taking Jesus at His word.

However the Roman Catholic authorities use the various passages detailing the Last Supper and the institution of the Lord's Supper as their proof texts. Those passages are Matthew 26:26-28, Mark 14:22-24, Luke

22:19-20, and 1 Corinthians 11:23-29. Let's look at the last one, where Paul wrote:

> For I have received of the Lord that which also I have delivered unto you, That the Lord Jesus the same night in which he was betrayed, took bread: And when he had given thanks, he brake it, and said, Take, eat: this is my body, which is broken for you: this do in remembrance of me. After the same manner also he took the cup, when he had supped, saying, This cup is the new testament in my blood: this do ye, as oft as ye drink it, in remembrance of me. For as often as ye eat this bread, and drink this cup, ye do shew the Lord's death till he come. Wherefore whosoever shall eat this bread, and drink this cup of the Lord, unworthily, shall be guilty of the body and blood of the Lord. But let a man examine himself, and so let him eat of that bread and drink of that cup. For he that eateth and drinketh unworthily, eateth and drinketh damnation to himself, not discerning the Lord's body.

It is true that Jesus said, "This is my body" and "This is my blood." He said this as He was there bodily in the midst of His apostles. It is truly a beautiful example of figurative language, and considering what He was about to undergo, His death and resurrection, it takes on an even greater significance. But the fact remains that it was an example of figurative language. The very fact that He was physically there saying these words and handing the bread and fruit of the vine to His apostles illustrates this point.

There is another example of our Lord using figurative language in John 10:1-10. Two times in that passage Jesus said, "I am the door." Did He mean a literal door, one that you can open and walk through? Did He mean a door like the ones that we have in our homes? No, that was figurative language meant to convey a message. To attempt to force a literal, physical interpretation upon it is to pervert the passage.

Another passage often referred to in defense of transubstantiation by the Roman Catholics is John 6:48-58. In this passage Jesus said that He was the "bread of life." We will begin reading in verse 51:

> I am the living bread which came down from heaven: if any man eat of this bread, he shall live forever: and the bread that I will give is my flesh, which I will give for the life of the world. The Jews therefore strove among themselves, saying, How can this man give us his flesh to eat? Then Jesus said unto them, Verily, verily, I say unto you, Except ye eat the flesh of the Son of man, and drink his blood, ye have no life in you. Whoso eateth my flesh and drinketh my blood, hath eternal life; and I will raise him up at the last day. For my flesh is meat indeed, and my blood is drink indeed. He that eateth my flesh, and

drinketh my blood, dwelleth in me, and I in him. As the living Father hath sent me, and I live by the Father: so he that eateth me, even he shall live by me. This is that bread which came down from heaven: not as your fathers did eat manna, and are dead: he that eateth of this bread shall live forever.

Viewing this passage literally, as the Roman Catholic authorities do, is to make the same mistake the Jews who originally heard it made. They thought that He actually meant to eat His flesh and to drink His blood. "From that time many of his disciples went back, and walked no more with him" (John 6:66). But they were applying a physical meaning to a spiritual message, and Jesus explained in verse 63 that His words were not meant to be taken literally: "It is the spirit that quickeneth: the flesh profiteth nothing; the words that I speak unto you, they are spirit, and they are life." Thus, the eating is not literal, any more than the bread is literal or the flesh. The same is true of the drinking and the blood. We partake of that bread, or of Him who came down from heaven, by hearing of Him, believing on Him, and being united with Him in obedience to His commands. By becoming His disciples, learning of Him and following Him in all things, we figuratively eat His flesh and drink His blood. We assimilate, accept, and devote ourselves to Jesus. Jesus Himself denied the literal interpretation, and in so doing denied the doctrine of transubstantiation.

Theological Gobbledegook

I am aware that many have vehemently opposed transubstantiation, and some in their zealousness have even called it a form of cannibalism. But that is not the point. If our Lord has instructed us to do something, then we are to do it, regardless of what it might be. But our Lord did not teach the doctrine of transubstantiation, the early church did not believe or practice it, and it took the Roman Catholic authorities 1200 years to definitely state it. It is another instance of a gradual development of a doctrine in the minds of men, which the Roman Catholic authorities presume to present as having been taught by the Lord. While it is tedious reading, allow me to present the theological argument used by Roman Catholic authorities to support *their doctrine*, and you can determine for yourselves if this is from the mind of God or from the wandering imaginations of men. It almost makes you wonder, which came first—the doctrine, or the reasoning that is supposed to support it.

From the book, *The Roman Catholic Church*, by John L. McKenzie, S.J., and bearing the Imprimatur of Joseph P. O'Brien, S.T.D., Vicar General of the Archdiocese of New York, we find:

Since the Fourth Council of the Lateran (1215), the official word for the sacramental change is transubstantiation, a rather barbarous term both in Latin and English. As the Council defined it, it means that the entire substance of the bread is changed into the substance of the body of Christ, and the entire substance of the wine into the blood of Christ, with only the species of bread and wine remaining. The Latin word *species* here would normally be translated "appearances," but in the cautious language of Roman Catholic theology the Latin words usually goes into English as *species*, and thus becomes unintelligible to the untrained. *The Catholic assertion is based on the Aristotelian and medieval philosophy of substance and accident, defined in the schools respectively as that which exists in itself (substance) and that which exists in something else (accident).* The bread and wine become substantially something else, but accidentally they are unchanged. Thus the body and blood of Christ are not seen, touched, or tasted; no substance is the object of the senses. But what is present is the substance, for only a substance can be present. The body and blood of Christ do not take on the sensible qualities of bread and wine. The body of Christ is neither expanded nor contracted nor moved from place to place; it simply becomes present where the transubstantiation has been effected by the sacramental formula. It is not present in the same manner (called in the schools local presence) as it was present in Galilee, however; it is present as a substance. *To illustrate, my own presence in this office is not due to my substantial reality, but to the commensuration of my extension with the extension of the place where I sit* (148).

If this came from the mind of God, why is it necessary for the Catholic assertion to be based on the Aristotelian and medieval philosophy of substance and accident? Truly, this is an example of theological gobbledegook. If God's word had taught it, we could understand. Since God's word does not teach transubstantiation, Roman Catholic authorities must turn to theology to make their case.

Purgatory

One of the fundamental beliefs of Roman Catholicism is the existence of an intermediate state called Purgatory. As a young boy growing up in the parochial school system, I was indoctrinated with this belief and accepted it with little or no question. Only as I grew and found out that most of the religious bodies in the world which claim to worship Jesus did not believe in Purgatory did I begin to examine for myself. What I discovered surprised me, and I am sure would surprise many of the Roman Catholic laity if they would take the time and expend the energy to examine for themselves.

What Is Purgatory?

As usual we will allow the Catholic writers to define the subject for us. In *The Baltimore Catechism* we find this question and answer:

> What is Purgatory? Purgatory is a state in which those suffer for a time who die guilty of venial sins, or without having satisfied for the punishment due to their sins. The Bible says that nothing defiled shall enter into Heaven (Apoc. 21:27 or Rev. 21:27). Will those, who at death are not spotlessly holy, have to go to Hell? Christ says no, because many will be forgiven in the next world (Matt. 12:32). There is therefore a place of cleansing in the next world, and this place we call Purgatory. Hell is only for those who die as enemies of God (III, #62).

To further define the subject, we turn to the book, *Twenty-Five Questions Non-Catholics Ask*, by Rev. John A. O'Brien, bearing the Nihil Obstat of Edward A. Miller and the Imprimatur of Leo A. Pursley:

> The word Purgatory does not occur in Scripture, but the reality it symbolizes is referred to both in the Old and the New Testament and in the writing of the Fathers in the East and in the West. Since the belief in the efficacy of prayers for the dead was *universal in the infant Church*, it follows that *the belief in Purgatory*

was likewise universal; for without a Purgatory, prayers for the dead would be meaningless.

So, by combining what we have read, we can determine that Purgatory, according to Catholic writers, is a state between death and our eternal reward, in which those who died guilty of venial sins or without having satisfied the punishment due for their sins, are cleansed by means of punishment. While the word Purgatory does not appear in the Scriptures, the reality behind it is said to be taught in the Old and New Testaments, as well as in the writings of the early church Fathers. We are told that the infant church universally believed in the efficacy of prayers for the dead and that it naturally follows that they also universally believed in Purgatory.

Our task is to determine whether or not such a place as Purgatory actually exists, whether or not it was believed to have existed by the "infant church" the world over, and whether or not it is taught in the Scriptures, either by a direct statement to that effect or by implication. According to the Roman Catholic authorities, the answer to each one of our inquiries should be "yes." We will see.

When Did the Doctrine Begin?

Very early after the death of the last of the apostles, we begin to find germs of this doctrine. In the writings of Marcion and in the Shepherd of Hermes, both of which can be dated in the second century, we find the idea of an abode of the dead in which their eternal destinies can be changed. Then in the writings of Origen, a learned third-century early church figure who died in A.D. 254 we read:

> For if on the foundation of Christ you have built not only gold and silver and precious stones (1 Cor. 3) but also wood and hay and stubble, what do you expect when the soul shall be separated from the body? Would you enter into heaven with your wood and hay and stubble and thus defile the kingdom of God . . . ? It remains then that you be committed to the fire, which will burn the light materials. . . . But this fire consumes not the creature, but what the creature has himself built. . . . It is manifest that the fire destroys the wood of our transgressions, and then returns to us the reward of our good works (13, 445, 448).

Little is found concerning this subject after Origen with the exception of some statements about it from Gregory of Nyssa and Ambrose, both from the fourth century. Then came the noted theologian, Augustine, in the fifth century. He gave the doctrine of Purgatory definite form, but expressed doubts about it himself. Augustine said in his writing, *Enchiridion:*

The question whether such is the case is justified and may yield to a solution *or remain in doubt: the question whether some of the faithful are saved by a sort of purgatorial fire,* and this sooner or later according as they have loved more or less the goods that perish (69).

It remained for Gregory the Great, who held the office of Pope from A.D. 590-604, to formally define and shape the doctrine. This he did in his sixth-century work, *Dialogue.* Gregory wrote:

> It is to be believed that before the judgment there is a purgatorial fire for certain minor sins. For the Truth says that if anyone blasphemes against the Holy Ghost, it shall not be forgiven him, either in this world or in the next. From which we learn that certain sins may be forgiven in this world and certainly in the next. . . . We must know, however, that a man will not be cleansed in purgatory of even the least sins, unless during his lifetime he deserved by his good works to receive such favor (4, 39).

About 900 years later the doctrine was decreed an article of faith by the Council of Florence. This can be found in *Laetentur Coeli,* 1439. Then 124 years later, due to the public outrage surrounding the sale of indulgences, which is tied so closely to the idea of Purgatory, the Council of Trent confirmed the doctrine. On December 3, 1563, in the *Decree of the Council of Trent,* Session 25, the Council decreed:

> Whereas the Catholic Church, instructed by the Holy Ghost, has from the sacred writings and the ancient tradition of the fathers taught in sacred councils and very recently in this oecumenical synod that there is a purgatory, and that the souls there detained are helped by the suffrages of the faithful, but principally by the acceptable sacrifice of the altar; the holy synods enjoins on bishops that they diligently endeavor that the sound doctrine concerning purgatory, transmitted by the holy fathers and sacred councils, be believed, maintained, taught, and everywhere proclaimed by the faithful of Christ.

So that details the historical development of the doctrine of Purgatory. It is interesting to notice some of the flights of imagination the Catholic clergy has engaged in over the years, particularly during the Middle Ages. For instance, in *Systematic Theology* by Dr. Charles Hodge we read, "The Franciscans claimed that the head of their order descended annually into purgatory, and delivered all the brotherhood who were detained there. The Carmelites asserted that the Virgin Mary had promised that no one who died with the Carmelite scapulary upon their shoulders, should ever be lost" (III: 770).

The point is this—over 100 years after the time of Christ we find the first inkling of the idea behind the doctrine of Purgatory. Over 200 years after Christ, Origen writes concerning an intermediate state of cleansing. Approximately 400 years after the time of Christ, the greatest theologian the Catholic Church had to offer, Augustine, began to give definite form to the doctrine, but did himself doubt parts of it. Almost 600 years after the time of Christ, Gregory the Great, the architect of the medieval papacy, formally defined and shaped the doctrine. Over 1400 years after the time of Christ, the doctrine was decreed an article of faith, and over 1500 years after Christ, the doctrine was officially confirmed. *There is simply no way that it can truthfully be said that the "infant church" universally believed in Purgatory. History proves that that is undeniably false.* We have seen that it took the Catholic officials 600 years to sufficiently discover this so-called biblical doctrine to formally define and shape it, and 1500 years to officially confirm it. This is not a doctrine that originated with Christ; it is a doctrine that evolved in the minds of men over a 1500-year period. About such things Jesus *did* say, "But in vain they do worship me, teaching for doctrines the commandments of men" (Matt. 15:9).

> **There is simply no way that it can truthfully be said that the "infant church" universally believed in Purgatory. History proves that that is undeniably false.**

Scriptural Support For Purgatory?

As the Catholic authorities seek to find some sort of scriptural support for their doctrine, they will cite a number of New Testament passages. Their main ones are Matthew 12:32, 1 Corinthians 3:13-15, Jude 22-23 and 1 Peter 3:18-20. None of these passages mentions Purgatory or even implies the doctrine. To get such an idea from these passages requires incredible assumptions on the part of the reader and requires that other New Testament passages that refute such an idea as Purgatory be ignored.

The primary scriptural support cited by the Roman Catholic authorities is found in 2 Maccabees 12:39-45. 2 Maccabees is an Old Testament book found in the Catholic Bible. It was not accepted by the Jews as being inspired and was written after their Bible was completed. It is an apocryphal book and is accepted only by the Catholic authorities. Here is what this passage says:

> And the day following Judas came with his company, to take away the bodies of them that had been slain, and to bury them with their kinsmen, in the

sepulchers of their fathers. *And they found under the coats of the slain some of the donaries of the idols of Jamnia, which the law forbiddeth to the Jews:* so that all plainly saw, that for this cause they were slain. Then they all blessed the just judgment of the Lord, who had discovered the things that were hidden. And so betaking themselves to prayers, they besought him, that the sin which had been committed might be forgiven. But the most valiant Judas exhorted the people to keep themselves from sin, forsasmuch as they saw before their eyes what had happened, because of the sins of those that were slain. And making a great gathering, he sent twelve thousand drachmas of silver to Jerusalem for a sacrifice to be offered for the sins of the dead, thinking well and religiously concerning the resurrection. For if he had not hoped that they that were slain should rise again, it would have seemed superfluous and vain to pray for the dead. And because he considered that they who had fallen asleep with godliness, had great grace laid up for them. It is therefore a holy and wholesome thought to pray for the dead that they may be loosed from sins.

I find nothing here about an intermediate state of suffering for those who died with venial sins or still owing punishment for sins already forgiven. I find mention of prayers for the dead, and from that the doctrine of Purgatory is to be inferred? Besides, these dead were guilty of the sin of idolatry. Their death was a judgment of God according to the passage. Idolatry is a *mortal sin* according to Catholicism. Those dying in mortal sin do not go to Purgatory. This passage either proves too much as far as Purgatory is concerned, or nothing at all.

So the primary scriptural support for Purgatory offered by the Catholic authorities is an apocryphal book, accepted by no one other than Catholics, and the passage cited does not refer to Purgatory. Indeed, it cannot, based upon their own definition of who is to go there. This is mighty slim support for such an important doctrine.

The Catholic doctrine of Purgatory cannot be supported, either scripturally or historically.

Mortal and Venial Sin

One of the most interesting doctrines of Roman Catholicism concerns the subject of sin and the distinction that the Catholic Church makes between what they call "mortal sin" and "venial sin." Around this distinction between sins has grown up an entire system of what is called "Moral Theology." It was inevitable that such would occur, because in actual practice this doctrine of mortal and venial sins is not quite as clear as it may appear to be at first glance. There are too many sins that do not clearly belong in one category or another, there are too many gray areas, and consequently, Roman Catholic theologians have addressed themselves to this problem. The result of their studies is a system of "Moral Theology" that is at once arbitrary and manmade. It is a system that cries out for the simplicity of God's revealed Word.

Let us begin by saying that God's Word makes no such "mortal-venial" distinction between sins. It does not categorize some as being more serious than others. God's Word simply says, "For all have sinned, and come short of the glory of God" (Rom. 3:23). God's Word further reveals, "For the wages of sin is death; but the gift of God is eternal life through Jesus Christ our Lord" (Rom. 6:23). Any sin, unrepented of, will result in eternal damnation. There are not some that will bring about this result and others that won't. Any unrepented of sin will have the same result.

In Romans 1:29-32, there are several sins listed, some of which would be called venial and others which would be called mortal under the Catholic system; yet God's Word makes no such distinction. The ultimate result of all of them is the same. Paul wrote in that passage:

> Being filled with all unrighteousness, fornication, wickedness, covetousness, maliciousness; full of envy, murder, debate, deceit, malignity; whisperers, back-

biters, haters of God, despiteful, proud, boasters, inventors of evil things, disobedient to parents, Without understanding, covenant breakers, without natural affection, implacable, unmerciful: Who knowing the judgment of God, that they which commit such things are worthy of death, not only do the same, but have pleasure in them that do them.

So the true Bible believer does not accept this Roman Catholic distinction because it is nowhere found in God's Word.

But what, then, is this Roman Catholic distinction, and what are some of the problems that it leads to? I will be referring to a Roman Catholic college textbook entitled, *College Moral Theology*, written in 1958 by Anthony F. Alexander, Department of Religion at John Carroll University. The book bears the Nihil Obstat of Rev. Joseph T. Mangan, S.J., and the Imprimatur of Samuel Cardinal Stritch, D.D. The stated purpose of the book is "the moral formation of Catholic youth." Let's let the system speak for itself:

> 50. A mortal sin is a complete disruption of the moral order, which God has commanded us to follow to reach our goal in life. All legitimate authority comes from God. Every mortal sin is in some way a rebellion against God's authority. The attack may be on a law directly laid down by God as is the case of breaking the natural or positive divine law... The attack may constitute an indirect invasion of God's authority as the breaking of an ecclesiastical law. God has seen fit to invest certain organizations such as the Church and the state with His authority to impose penalties on those who break their laws. These governments can, if they wish, make their just laws bind under pain of sin. To break them seriously is then an indirect attack on God's authority (33).

> 51. The malice of a mortal sin lies in the fact that by it one completely rejects God in favor of a forbidden creature, which one cannot possess simultaneously with the love of God. . . .Example: Meat in itself is not bad. But the sin of a Catholic who eats meat on Friday lies in the fact that he implicitly tells God that he would rather have it than God's love and friendship. His preference and his rejection are embodied in a single deliberate choice (34).

It is interesting to note that the Roman Catholic hierarchy no longer requires American Roman Catholics to abstain from meat on Fridays. That which was once a mortal sin is no longer even a venial sin under this totally arbitrary system. One is forced to wonder what happened to those who died with the mortal sin of eating meat on Fridays, unforgiven.

54. Sins differ from each other in kind when they are violations of different commandments or different virtues. . . .A forbidden act can have as many malices as the number of Commandments it breaks. A single act may break a single Commandment and so be a sin of single malice. It may constitute a simultaneous attack on two or even three Commandments and so be a sin of double or triple malice. All the seriously sinful malices of an act must be removed before one can recover sanctifying grace (36).

55. One who departs this life in mortal sin is immediately condemned to hell; he there suffers the terrible frustration of having eternally lost his goal in life and the happiness which God had intended for him (36).

Now let's turn our attention to venial sins:

56. A venial sin constitutes a blameworthy delay in making progress towards God: it does not constitute a rejection of God in favor of a seriously forbidden object. A venial sin is essentially different from a mortal sin. In a venial sin the forbidden object is small enough to co-exist with the love of God (37).

57. It is possible to commit a venial sin by freely and deliberately choosing a slightly evil object (38).

58. It is possible to commit a venial sin by choosing an object which in itself is seriously forbidden but the choice is made by an imperfect human act (38).

It is important that I present here the example given in this case to show the ridiculousness of this system of theology in practice. In example number 58 the writer says, "There is a row of cheaply priced books on a shelf in a second-hand bookstore. Instead of buying a certain book, James steals it. It is really a valuable first edition but until he learns its real value, he is guilty of only a venial sin."

So you can see that under the Roman Catholic system of moral theology, it is not the stealing itself but the value of that which was stolen that determines the seriousness of the sin. Under God's Law, all stealing is serious, period, with the value of that which was stolen bearing no weight at all as far as the ultimate result is concerned if the sin of stealing is not repented of.

59. Those who depart this life in venial sin or who must satisfy for temporal punishment due to sin, go to purgatory: before being admitted to heaven, they undergo great suffering caused principally by their delay in seeing God (39).

This then is the Roman Catholic distinction between mortal and venial sins. Already we can get an inkling of the arbitrariness of this system. But again it is important that we let Roman Catholic authorities speak for themselves. So let's notice further how they put this system into practice:

8. The gravity of an injustice against an individual involving material goods is determined according to a relative standard. The existence of a relative standard can be proved. Different individuals have different obligations according to their state in life. The obligations of some are more pressing and more numerous than others depending on such factors as number of children or condition of health. Varied sums are needed to meet varied sizes of obligations. Some can afford less a loss than others. This standard is called relative because it varies from person to person. . . .The commonly accepted verdict is that it is a mortal sin to deprive a person and his family of the amount needed for a day's upkeep. Several factors can cause variation in this. The student is to notice that a day's upkeep is not the same as a day's wages, for one must live even on the days that he does not work. It is a week's wages divided by seven. To steal a less amount is a venial sin. EXAMPLE: To steal over $2.00 from a widow drawing a monthly pension check of $60.00 is a mortal sin. To steal about $7.00 from a wage-earner who works five days a week at $10.00 per day is a mortal sin (203-204).

10. If a person takes temporal goods in a series of venial thefts, he steals the amount necessary for a mortal sin when the stolen amounts add up to twice the amount set down in the relative or absolute standards (205).

14. The gravity of the guilt of a person who has committed an injustice is determined on the basis of the knowledge which he had when he made his choice to commit the wrong. Sin is committed when one chooses what he knows to be a seriously forbidden object. If one takes an object of notable value while unsuspectingly believing that it is of slight value, he then commits a venial sin. But if he later comes to know its great value, he commits a mortal sin at the moment that he intends to keep doing it (208).

On and on we could go, giving example after example from their own writings, indeed from the very textbook used for teaching moral theology in Roman Catholic Universities. But these few statements are sufficient to show that the mortal-venial distinction and the accompanying moral theology as taught by Roman Catholicism is not of God. It is completely arbitrary and totally manmade.

The Sacrament of Penance— Going to Confession

I confess to the Almighty God, to the blessed Virgin Mary, to blessed Michael the Archangel, to blessed John the Baptist, to the holy apostles Peter and Paul, to all the saints, and to you, father, that I have sinned exceedingly, in thought, word, and deed, through my fault, through my fault, through my most grievous fault.

With these words I began my early confessions as a child to one of the parish priests of St. John's the Evangelist. This was the prescribed formula for confession at the time. Later it was changed to, "Bless me, father, for I have sinned. It has been _____ months since my last confession. My sins are. . . ."

After the initial statement I would then list my sins to the priest, make the Act of Contrition, and await the absolution and penance assigned me from the priest. All of this took place inside a small box, or closet-like structure located within the church building. Having made my confession, received absolution, and performed my penance, I could leave the building confident of having had my sins forgiven and once again being in proper standing with the Holy Mother Church. Those outside of the Roman Catholic Church did not understand the significance of Confession. They imagined strange and unjust things about the confessional, and they unjustly questioned the motives of the priests. After all, I had been taught that penance was a sacrament instituted by Christ, that the practice of auricular confession (so called because the sins are whispered secretly into the ear of the priest), was something that had been done by the Church from the beginning, and that the priest was empowered by God to forgive me all of my sins. Further study in the years since that time has demonstrated to me that what I was taught was not true.

The Historical Development

One may search the Scriptures from cover to cover and find no indication of the practice of auricular confession at all. One may search through the writings of the first 1,000 years of the church and still find no authorization or indication of such a practice being used. Still further, one may diligently examine the writings of such men as Chrysostom, Athanasius, Nestorius, Tertullian, Jerome, Origen, even Augustine, and come to the conclusion that these men, who wrote a great deal about the practices and beliefs of their time, lived and died without ever going to an auricular confession, or even thinking about it. There is no indication anywhere that for the first 1,000 years after the death of Christ, Christians were required to come on bended knee before a priest and secretly confess their sins to him. Such was unheard of and was no part of the practice of early Christians.

One may search the Scriptures from cover to cover and find no indication of the practice of auricular confession at all.

There are indications that by the fifth century confession had been introduced into the church on a voluntary basis. This was done by the authority of Leo the Great, a man most noted for his meeting with Attila the Hun at Mantua and the agreement he reached with him (*The Catholic Layman's Library*). However, it was not until the Fourth Lateran Council in A.D. 1215, under the leadership of Innocent III, that auricular confession was made mandatory for all Catholics. This council decreed that once a year Catholics were required to confess and seek absolution from a priest. This decree was later reconfirmed by the Council of Trent, Session 14, from November 25, 1551. The wording of the statement from the Council of Trent is interesting in light of historical fact. They wrote:

> If any one denieth either that sacramental confession was instituted or is necessary to salvation of divine right; or saith that the manner of confessing secretly to a priest alone, *which the Church hath ever observed from the beginning* and doth observe, is alien from the institution and command of Christ, and is a human invention; let him be anathema (Canon 6).

What the Council of Trent said is simply not true. The "manner of confessing secretly to a priest alone" was not observed by the church from the beginning. A very simple look through the early history of the church shows this to be false. Interestingly enough, Catholic authorities know that the statement of the Council of Trent is not true. In the Decree Promulgating the New Order of Penance in *Reconciliationem* by Paul VI on December 2, 1973 we find:

> Because of human weaknesses, however, it happens that Christians "abandon the love they had at first" (Apoc. 2:4) and by sinning break the links of friendship that bind them to God. For this reason, the Lord instituted a special sacrament for the remission of sins committed after Baptism (see John 20:21-23). *The Church has celebrated this sacrament through the ages, in various ways indeed, but always retaining its essential elements.*

Now either Paul VI is right, or the Council of Trent is right, or they are both wrong. Paul said that the sacrament of penance was performed by the church in "various ways." The Council of Trent said that the manner of confessing secretly to a priest had "ever been observed by the church from the beginning."

History clearly shows that the sacrament of penance, including auricular confession, was not instituted by Christ but is a manmade invention that was not enjoined upon Catholic people until A.D. 1215, almost 1200 years after the death of Christ.

Modern Practice

Even with the sweeping changes in practice brought about in the Roman Catholic Church by Vatican II, the practice of penance remains an archaic, manmade institution. *The Catholic Layman's Library* gives this description of present-day auricular confession:

> In the present penitential liturgy in most of the English-speaking churches the penitent asks the priest's blessing, tells how long it is since his last confession, confesses his sins according to kind and number, receives words of encouragement from the priest, hears the words of forgiveness pronounced over him when he has expressed his sorrow, and then performs the works of satisfaction imposed by the priest (848).

All of this takes place within the confessional. *The New Code of Canon Law* that took effect in 1983 contains thirty-three canons that deal directly with this practice. Included in them is Canon 965, which states, "Only a priest is the minister of the sacrament of penance." Canon 964 gives instructions concerning the location of the confessional grille that is to be fixed between the priest and the penitent. Canon 989 obliges each Catholic having attained the age of discretion to confess serious sins at least once a year. These are just three of the thirty-three different canons concerning this practice.

The point that I would want all Roman Catholics to understand is that the whole idea of auricular confession is manmade and completely foreign to God's way. No man on earth possesses the power to forgive sins or not forgive sins as he chooses. 1 Peter 2:9 teaches that all Christians are priests. 1 John 1:9 teaches that we are to confess our faults to God, and He will forgive us. 1Timothy 2:5 teaches that there is but one mediator between God and men, and that mediator is Christ Jesus. Penance, as a sacrament, and auricular confession sprang from the minds of the Roman Catholic hierarchy and serves only them.

Am I Good Enough To Go To Heaven?

There is a charge that is often leveled against the Roman Catholic Church concerning their official teaching related to salvation and man's part in it. They are often charged with teaching salvation by works or by merit, meaning that I will get into heaven if I am good enough to get there. I suppose that the vitally important question in such a discussion is this: Just exactly what does Roman Catholicism teach about man's part in salvation? Do they teach the idea of meritorious works whereby man can "earn" his salvation? If Roman Catholic authorities do teach salvation by works, then it needs to be exposed. If they do not teach such a thing, then those making the charges against them need to stop.

As should always be the case, let us allow Roman Catholic writers to explain their position to us. In the book, *The Question Box*, we find this question and answer:

> What constitutes the Sacrament of Penance? On the part of the priest the absolution, "I absolve thee from thy sins in the name of the Father and of the Son and of the Holy Ghost." On the part of the penitent, contrition, i.e., sorrow of heart and detestation of sin committed, with the resolve to sin no more; confession, i.e., the declaration of sins to a priest with the purpose of obtaining forgiveness; and satisfaction, i.e., *the payment of the temporal punishment due forgiven sins* (280).

All of these elements are necessary, according to the Roman Catholic Church, for forgiveness of sins to truly take place. There is the absolution, the contrition, confession, and the payment of satisfaction. Now obviously in a discussion of salvation by works, we must focus upon that "satisfaction" or "the payment of the temporal punishment due forgiven sins." Just exactly what is that and where does it come from?

In *The Catechism of the Catholic Church*, we find, "Jesus' call to conversion and penance, like that of the prophets before him, does not aim first at outward works, 'sackcloth and ashes,' fasting and mortification, but at the conversion of the heart, interior conversion. Without this, such penances remain sterile and false; however, *interior conversion urges expression in visible signs, gestures and works of penance* (1430).

Thus we see this "interior conversion" manifesting itself, or "urging expression" in outward, visible signs, gestures, and works of penance. But are these outward signs, gestures, and works of penance necessary, and are they efficacious in obtaining salvation?

Again, from *The Catechism of the Catholic Church* we find:

The interior penance of the Christian can be expressed in many and various ways. Scripture and the Fathers insist above all on three forms, fasting, prayer, and almsgiving, which express conversion in relation to oneself, to God, and to others. Alongside the radical purification brought about by Baptism or martyrdom *they cite as means of obtaining forgiveness of sins*: efforts at reconciliation with one's neighbor, tears of repentance, concern for the salvation of one's neighbor, the intercession of the saints, and the practice of charity, *'which covers a multitude of sins'* (1434).

How Does the Roman Catholic Church View Sin?

Before we go any further in our discussion we need to explain the Roman Catholic view of sin and its consequences. It is in one of the consequences of sin that the matter of meritorious works enters in. The Roman Catholic Church teaches that sin has a double consequence. Again, from *The Catechism of the Catholic Church* we find:

Grave sin deprives us of communion with God and therefore makes us incapable of eternal life, the privation of which is called the "eternal punishment" of sin. On the other hand, every sin, even venial, entails an unhealthy attachment to creatures, which must be purified either here on earth, or after death in the state called Purgatory. This purification frees one from what is called the "temporal punishment" of sin. These two punishments must not be conceived of as a kind of vengeance inflicted by God from without, but as following from the very nature of sin. A conversion which proceeds from a fervent charity can attain the complete purification of the sinner in such a way that no punishment would remain. The forgiveness of sins and restoration of communion with God entail the remission of the eternal punishment of sins, but temporal punishment of sin remains. While patiently bearing sufferings and trials of all kinds and, when the day comes, serenely facing death, the Christian must strive to accept this temporal punishment of sins as a grace. He should strive by works of mercy and charity, as well as by prayer and the various practices of penance, to put off completely the "old man" and to put on the "new man" (1472).

Thus, in the Roman Catholic Church, a grave sin (or mortal sin) carries with it not only the loss of communion with God and the incapability of eternal life, but also carries with it "temporal punishment." Even a venial sin (which, according to their doctrine, does not separate one from God) carries with it "temporal punishment." This temporal punishment is what makes up the second part of the double consequence of sin. The works of merit that a person performs (and which lead individuals to rightly say that the Catholic Church teaches salvation by works) affects the temporal punishment. You see, purification must take place, and it will either take place here on earth or after death in purgatory. By various works of merit an individual receives an increase in sanctifying grace and frees himself of a proportional amount of temporal punishment. *What the works of merit affect is not the forgiveness of the sins, but the amount of temporal punishment due on account of sin.*

How does this affect work, or how does it take place according to Catholic theology? I have in my possession a textbook that has been used in various Roman Catholic colleges entitled, *College Moral Theology*, from which comes the following quote:

> The actions from which we can gain merit must be human, morally good, and must flow from supernaturalized powers. The first requisite of an act capable of being meritorious is that it must be a human act. No one can make progress towards his goal unless he chooses it, turns toward it, and pursues it. To do this, a person must have control of his act. The second requisite is that it must be morally good. No one reaches a goal unless he travels along the correct route. The route toward our goal is fixed and stable. It is the moral law, which God has laid down for all to follow. The third requisite is that the agent be in the state of grace. When an act has these qualities, it is capable of gaining merit. God has promised a supernatural reward for these acts of His adoptive children. . . . Every good work of the just man merits some increase of grace. We are speaking here of merit in the strict sense of the word. Merit that gives a right to a reward. This merit is due these acts because God has promised it. Besides, being done under the influence of grace they have a superior value. They are also performed in His service (at least implicitly or virtually). Therefore, there

is some proportion between these acts and their supernatural reward, which is an increase of sanctifying grace here below and a consequent increase of heavenly glory. We can gain sanctifying grace only while we can choose or reject God; that is, while we live on earth. Our opportunity to amass grace ends with death. . . .A person who departs this life with only sanctifying grace on his soul goes immediately to heaven (46, 48-49).

Now let's see if we might make some sense of all this. According to Roman Catholic theology, a person who is not completely separated from God (and this would be a person who does not have unforgiven grave or mortal sins) freely chooses to perform a good work. Every good work of that individual gives him a right to a reward because God has promised such. That reward is a proportionate amount of sanctifying grace, and sanctifying grace gives the individual the right to heaven (*The New Baltimore Catechism*, #3, 62). The only thing standing between the individual who is in a state of grace (not completely separated from God) and heaven is the temporal punishment due his forgiven sins. Therefore, when he performs a good work he receives a proportional amount of sanctifying grace. That grace gives him the right to heaven; thus, a proportional amount of the temporal punishment he owes is taken away, remitted, by his performing that good work.

How does this work? From *The Catechism of the Catholic Church* we quote:

> In the communion of the saints, a perennial link of charity exists between the faithful who have already reached their heavenly home, those who are expiating their sins in purgatory and those who are still pilgrims on earth. Between them there is, too, an abundant exchange of all good things. In this wonderful exchange, the holiness of one profits others, well beyond the harm that the sin of one could cause others. Thus, recourse to the communion of the saints lets the contrite sinner be more promptly and efficaciously purified of the punishments for sin (1475).

> We also call these spiritual goods of the communion of saints the Church's treasury, which is not the sum total of the material goods which have accumulated during the course of the centuries. On the contrary, the treasury of the Church is the infinite value, which can never be exhausted, which Christ's merits have before God. They were offered so that the whole of mankind could be set free from sin and attain communion with the Father. In Christ, the Redeemer himself, the satisfactions and merits of his Redemption exist and find their efficacy (1476).

This treasury includes as well the prayers and good works of the Blessed Virgin Mary. They are truly immense, unfathomable, and even pristine in their value before God. In the treasury, too, are the prayers and good works of all the saints, all those who have followed in the footsteps of Christ the Lord and by his grace have made their lives holy and carried out the mission the Father entrusted to them. In this way they *attained their own salvation* and at the same time cooperated in saving their brothers in the unity of the Mystical Body (1477).

An indulgence is obtained through the Church who, by virtue of the power of binding and loosing granted her by Christ Jesus, intervenes in favor of individual Christians and opens for them the treasury of the merits of Christ and the saints to obtain from the Father of mercies the remission of the temporal punishment due for their sins. Thus the Church does not want simply to come to the aid of these Christians, but also to spur them to works of devotion, penance, and charity (1478).

Let's try to explain this in language we can all understand. The Roman Catholic Church claims that the merits of the work of Jesus Christ, plus the merits of the Blessed Virgin Mary, her prayers and good works, undiminished by any penalty due to sin, as well as the merits of the saints, their prayers and good works, vastly exceed any temporal punishment which they might have incurred; all of these merits are stored and administered by the Church in the Treasury of Merit. When an individual performs a specific act to which an indulgence is attached, the Church dispenses the appropriate amount of merits from its treasury to remit the appropriate amount of temporal punishment due for the individual's forgiven sins. Thus, not only will the Roman Catholic's own good works get him or her into heaven quicker, but somebody else's good works can be applied as well.

What Does the Bible Say?

How does all of this compare with what the Bible actually teaches? First of all, what is the consequence of sin? I believe the clearest and simplest statement of sin's consequence is found in Isaiah 59:1-2 which says, "Behold, the Lord's hand is not shortened, that it cannot save; neither his ear heavy, that it cannot hear: But your iniquities have separated between you and your God, and your sins have hid his face from you, that he will not hear." When someone sins, he or she is separated from God. That separation is referred to as "death" by the Apostle Paul in Romans 6:23. It is a spiritual death to which Paul refers. Whereas prior to sinning, all individuals exist in a state of pristine communion with God, sin breaks that communion; the individual dies spiritually and will be lost eternally if the sin is not forgiven.

Second, it is incorrect to believe that all sin has the "double consequence." It is false to believe that every sin comes with a certain amount of temporal punishment due it, either here or in purgatory. The Christian who sins is taught to repent, confess his sins to God, and pray for forgiveness. This is found in Acts 8:22 and 1 John 1:9. The idea of certain acts having to be performed as "penance" is simply not found in the Scriptures. The idea of every sin having a certain amount of "temporal punishment" due for it is the same false impression that the Jews of the first century had. Many of them believed that all suffering was the direct result of some sin in the individual's life or in the life of the parents of the individual. Jesus corrected this.

> There were present at that season some that told him of the Galilaeans, whose blood Pilate had mingled with their sacrifices. And Jesus answering said unto them, Suppose ye that these Galilaeans were sinners above all the Galilaeans, because they suffered such things? I tell you, Nay; but, except ye repent, ye shall all likewise perish. Or those eighteen, upon whom the tower in Siloam fell, and slew them, think ye that they were sinners above all men that dwelt in Jerusalem? I tell you, Nay; but, except ye repent, ye shall all likewise perish (Luke 13:1-5).

There may be physical consequences of sin here on earth. For instance, a drunken driver may have an accident and horribly injure himself or kill someone else, and those are physical consequences to be paid. However, those physical consequences have nothing to do with whether or not a person can be forgiven, and once the sin is forgiven, all things related to it are remembered by the Lord no more. When the Lord forgives, He forgives.

Additionally, Ephesians 2:8-9 tell us, "For by grace are ye saved through faith; and that not of yourselves: it is the gift of God: Not of works, lest any man should boast." The passage simply says: (1) We are saved by grace through faith; (2) That it is not of ourselves but is a gift of God; (3) That we do not "merit" salvation through our own works, so there is no place for boasting.

In Titus 2:11-12 we find, "For the grace of God that bringeth salvation hath appeared to all men, teaching us that, denying ungodliness and worldly lusts, we should live soberly, righteously, and godly in this present world." You see, my friends, God's grace appears teaching. That teaching must be accepted by faith and the blessings promised will be appropriated when that teaching is obeyed. All my good works, while necessary to walk in the light of the Lord, are my duty to perform. The idea of them somehow lessening temporal punishment for sins already forgiven is a manmade fantasy.

Our Lord Jesus said, "But which of you, having a servant plowing or feeding cattle, will say unto him by and by, when he is come from the field, Go and sit down to meat? And will not rather say unto him, Make ready wherewith I may sup, and gird thyself, and serve me, till I have eaten and drunken; and afterward thou shalt eat and drink? Doth he thank that servant because he did the things that were commanded of him? I trow not. So likewise ye, when ye shall have done all those things which are commanded you, say, We are unprofitable servants: *we have done that which was our duty to do*" (Luke 17:7-10).

The idea of an indulgence is ludicrous, for there is no temporal punishment due forgiven sins. And the good or bad works of another individual do not directly affect my spiritual condition. Ezekiel made this pertinent point when he said, "The soul that sinneth, it shall die. The son shall not bear the iniquity of the father, neither shall the father bear the iniquity of the son: the righteousness of the righteous shall be upon him, and the wickedness of the wicked shall be upon him" (Ezek. 18:20).

Again, the idea of a "treasury of merit" to be administered by the church is nothing more than a figment of man's imagination.

Indulgences

We will now turn our attention to the development of the Catholic doctrine of Indulgences. As a starting point, we will allow the Catholic authorities to define the subject for us. In *The Revised Edition of the Baltimore Catechism* we find the following questions and answers:

> What is an indulgence? An indulgence does not take away sin. Neither does it take away the eternal punishment due to mortal sins. An indulgence can produce its effects in the soul only after sins are forgiven and, in the case of mortal sins, only after their eternal punishment is taken away. . . .By an indulgence, the Church merely wipes out or lessens the temporal punishment due to sins already forgiven. The Church from the beginning has granted indulgences.

"An indulgence is a remission before God of the temporal punishment due to sins whose guilt has already been forgiven. . . ."

> How many kinds of indulgences are there? There are two kinds of indulgences, plenary and partial.

> What is plenary indulgence? A plenary indulgence is the remission of all the temporal punishment due to our sins.

> What is a partial indulgence? A partial indulgence is the remission of part of the temporal punishment due to our sins (332-335).

The Catechism of the Catholic Church tells us, "An indulgence is a remission before God of the temporal punishment due to sins whose guilt has already been forgiven, which the faithful Christian who is duly disposed gains under certain prescribed conditions through the action of the Church which, as the minister of redemption, dispenses and applies with authority the treasury of the satisfactions of Christ and the saints. An indulgence is partial or plenary according as it removes either part or all of the temporal punishment due to sin. Indulgences may be applied to the living or the dead." Let me mention that the "treasury of the satisfactions of Christ and the saints" is also referred to as "The Treasury of the Church" and "Treasury of Merits" in the *Catholic Encyclopedia*.

Many non-Catholics, in writing about this subject, have misrepresented the facts. The Catholic authorities do not now teach that indulgences are a license to sin, as many have charged. They do not teach that an indulgence constitutes forgiveness for sins yet to be committed. They do not teach that an indulgence is forgiveness at all. However, because they do not *now* teach these things does not mean that the doctrine of indulgences has always been presented in the same way that it is now, nor does it mean that the doctrine of indulgences has not been used in the past by the Roman Catholic authorities in less than honorable ways. Our purpose will be to try to determine when this doctrine began to take shape and to notice some of the tremendous abuses of it over the ages—abuses that should never have taken place, and would not have taken place, in an infallible church led by an infallible leader.

How Did It Develop?

Contrary to the statement made in *The Baltimore Catechism*, there is no evidence that the church granted indulgences "from the beginning." The early church knew nothing of the practice but it developed gradually as various church leaders moved further and further away from the simple New Testament church. As the doctrine began to take shape, indulgences were initially applicable only to the living. In *Roman Catholicism* Pope Gelasius (A.D. 495) stated, "They demand that we should also bestow forgiveness of sins upon the dead. Plainly this is impossible for us, for it is said, 'What things soever ye shall bind upon earth.' Those who are no longer upon the earth He has reserved for His own judgment" (265). The statement of Pope Gelasius clearly places the dead in the hands of God and beyond the reach and power of the living.

In 1096, during the Synod of Clermont, Pope Urban II granted a plenary indulgence to all who would take part in the crusades. Pope Clement (1342-1352) proclaimed the idea of a Treasury of Merit. This permitted the Catholic Church to apply to others, "the infinite satisfaction of Jesus Christ and the superabundant satisfaction of the Blessed Virgin Mary and of the saints" (*The Baltimore Catechism*, 337). Finally, in his Bull of 1476, Pope Sixtus IV granted a plenary indulgence applicable to the souls in purgatory. From here on, indulgences have been considered helpful to both the living and the dead.

Abuses

With these developments in the doctrine of indulgences, the stage was set for widespread abuse—and the abuse came, with the pope right in the middle. When a church, a cathedral, a hospital, or a school needed to be built or maintained, indulgences were sold to finance it. The laity, mostly poor and uneducated people, were led to believe that their departed loved ones were languishing in the terrible pain of purgatory and that they could purchase their release with money. In his book, *Martin Luther, His Life and Work*, written by a Jesuit priest named Hartmann Grisar, bearing both the Nihil Obstat and the Imprimatur, we find, "The extent to which even the papal curia went, may be seen in the case of the indulgences granted by Leo X, the proceeds of which were intended for the construction of St. Peter's Basilica at Rome" (90).

It was out of this moneymaking scheme of Pope Leo X that one of the most famous quotes of the Reformation came. Leo sent his emissaries throughout Europe to raise money through the sale of indulgences. Some of these men were most enthusiastic in their work. One by the name of John Tetzel had an innovative way of making his sale. Again from *Martin Luther, His Life and Work*, we find, "It cannot be proved that he used the famous saw which has been attributed to him: 'As soon as money in the casket rings—The soul its flight from Purgatory wings,' *but in substance his words approximated the proverb*" (92).

These blatant abuses and fleecing of the poor prompted Luther to state in the eighty-sixth thesis of the ninety-five he posted on the cathedral door in Wittenburg, Germany, these words: "Why does not the pope build the basilica of St. Peter with his own money, rather than with that of the poor, seeing that he is wealthier today than the richest Croesus?" (*Martin Luther, His Life and Work*, 93).

While we would expect the Catholic authorities to vigorously condemn this practice of selling indulgences to raise money to build earthly buildings, that is absolutely not the case. While admitting abuses of indulgence sales, the *Catholic Encyclopedia* says:

However the picture is not altogether black. Not all the money collected on the occasion of an indulgence grant went to the purpose for which the indulgence was preached, but much of it did, as is evidenced by the number of monuments that still remain. The great cathedrals and monastic establishments were either built or kept in repair; schools and universities were founded and endowed; hospitals were maintained (484).

There is no confession of guilt for selling such a thing in the first place or for playing on the emotions of people--just an admittance that some of the money didn't go where it was supposed to.

How could these abuses have taken place in a church that claims to have the special guidance of the Holy Spirit to keep it from error? How could these abuses have happened in a church supposedly led by an infallible leader? Indeed, how could this infallible leader have set in motion the process from which these abuses arose?

Curtailing the Abuses

Actually, abuses surrounding the doctrine of indulgences began to occur long before Pope Sixtus IV issued his Papal Bull in 1476 making indulgences applicable to those in purgatory. As early as 1215 the Fourth Lateran Council had condemned the "abuses of trafficking in indulgences" (*Catholic Encyclopedia*, 484). However, this condemnation did not stem the tide of abuses.

After Martin Luther's thesis dealing specifically with the abuses connecting indulgences and the doctrine behind the practice itself, the Catholic authorities realized that the time for more drastic action had come. The issue was addressed at the famous Council of Trent. The Council took two steps concerning indulgences. The first was the reaffirmation of the church's right to grant indulgences and the retaining of the practice. In *Twenty-Five Questions Non-Catholics Ask* by John A. O'Brien, the official Catholic teaching on the subject was expressed in this fashion by the Council of Trent:

> Since the power of conferring indulgences was granted by Christ to the Church, and she has, even in the most ancient times, used this kind of power, delivered unto her of God; the Sacred Holy Synod teaches and enjoins that the use of indulgences, for the Christian people most salutary and approved of by the authority of the Sacred Councils, *is to be retained in the Church; and it condemns, with anathema, those who either assert they are useless, or who deny that there is in the Church the power of granting them* (79).

The second step taken by the Council of Trent was the enactment of certain disciplinary measures to correct the abuses surrounding the doctrine of indulgences, which they had just reaffirmed and retained. These disciplinary measures did not solve the problem. From the *Catholic Encyclopedia* we read:

> In the year 1567, St. Pius V *regretted that the measures taken by Trent had proved ineffective and accordingly struck at the root of the evil* by abrogating "every indulgence. . . .for which a helping hand must be offered, and which contains in any way whatsoever permission to make collections" (Bull Rom. 7:536, #484).

I personally find the reaction of the *Catholic Encyclopedia* to this action by Pius V to be most interesting. About his decree the *Catholic Encyclopedia* says, "The *drastic legislation* meant a *serious loss of revenue* to numerous churches, monasteries, hospitals, and other charitable foundations. Because of it, however, instances of indulgence 'traffic' became rare and are *today nonexistent*" (484). I find this interesting for two reasons. First, it constitutes an admittance of the fact that a primary reason for the sale of indulgences was to raise revenue for churches, monasteries, hospitals, and other charitable foundations. It is important that we keep this in mind. Second, it says that instances of indulgence "traffic" are nonexistent today. Such a statement deserves further attention.

Indulgence Traffic Nonexistent Today

It is proper to say that the sale of indulgences is today technically forbidden by the Catholic Church. It is equally safe to say that that rule has been violated on numerous occasions, and that the spirit of it has been violated on many, many more.

Pope John XXIII practiced the sale of indulgences openly. He was later condemned for it by the church council. Loraine Boettner states in his book, *Roman Catholicism*:

> The late Pope John XXIII, in 1958, granted a plenary indulgence to all who *attended* his coronation ceremony or listened by radio or viewed the ceremony on television or newsreel. And again, on Easter Sunday, 1961, he granted a plenary indulgence to all who *attended* the Easter observance in St. Peter's square in Rome (264).

The significance of this quote lies in the emphasis on attendance at these ceremonies. When people travel to St. Peter's in Rome and tour the Vatican, the amount of money brought into the coffers of the Roman Catholic Church is tremendous. Pope John Paul II declared 1983 as a Holy Year for the expressed purpose of attracting people to Rome to increase revenues.

Beyond these instances is the practice of having prayers and masses said for the souls of departed loved ones. Few participating Catholics who have their names on parish rolls have not received a letter from some Catholic organization or other, usually around All Saints Day, offering to include their dead loved one's name in special prayers or at a mass. I have yet to see one of these offers that does not include the mention of a "donation." This may not technically be "selling indulgences," but it is about as close as you can come. As a young child in Catholic schools, I was convinced that one of the nicest things I could do was to purchase a "bouquet" of masses for a dead grandmother or grandfather, and I did it. I now question the honesty of the leaders of an organization that will say they forbid the sale of indulgences and yet allow such things to go on. Indeed, they encourage them.

As a young child in Catholic schools, I was convinced that one of the nicest things I could do was to purchase a "bouquet" of masses for a dead grandmother or grandfather, and I did it.

"Vatican Will Allow Indulgences By TV"

The above title appeared in the December 19, 1985 edition of *The Cincinnati Enquirer*, and was followed by the following statement:

Rome – The Vatican, in an unusual shift in Roman Catholic devotional practice, said Wednesday that Catholics who follow the pope's annual Christmas benediction on television or radio will partake for the first time in the plenary indulgence reserved until now for those who were physically present at the service. Indulgences are a release by way of devotional practices from certain forms of punishment resulting from sin.

So by watching or listening to the pope's Christmas service, Roman Catholics the world over could have all of the temporal punishment due for their sins, the guilt of which had already been forgiven, taken away. If they were to die immediately after receiving this plenary indulgence, there would be no time in purgatory for them. This certainly sounds simple enough, but as is the case with all manmade religious doctrines, it is not as easy as it seems. I could not help but wonder how many Roman Catholics know what else was required of them by the teaching of their church to gain this "plenary indulgence."

One of the documents that came out of Vatican II was *Apostolic Constitution On the Revision of Indulgences.* It was authorized by Paul VI and was presented on January 1, 1967. Included in this *Constitution* were twenty "norms" concerning indulgences. Such things as the granting of them, the gaining of them, and the regulations concerning them were contained therein. I would like to present the first ten. They are:

1. An indulgence is a remission before God of the temporal punishment due to sins whose guilt has already been forgiven, which the faithful Christian who is duly disposed gains under *certain defined conditions* through the Church's help when, as minister of Redemption, she dispenses and applies with authority the treasury of the satisfaction won by Christ and the saints.

2. An indulgence is partial or plenary according as it removes either part or all of the temporal punishment due to sin.

3. Partial as well as plenary indulgences can always be applied to the dead by way of prayer.

4. From now on a partial indulgence will be indicated only with the words "partial indulgence" without any determination of days or years.

5. The faithful who at least with a contrite heart perform an action to which a partial indulgence is attached, obtain, in addition to the remission of temporal punishment merited by the action itself, an equal remission of punishment through the Church's intervention.

6. A plenary indulgence can be gained only once a day, except for the provision stated in n. 18 below for those who are "on the point of death." A partial indulgence can be gained more than once a day, unless there is an explicit direction to the contrary.

7. The requirements for gaining a plenary indulgence are: the indulgenced work must be performed and three conditions fulfilled. These are (a) sacramental confession, (b) eucharistic communion, (c) prayer for the Pope's intentions. Further, it is necessary to be free from all attachment to any sin at all, even venial sin. If this condition is not complete or if the conditions laid down are not fulfilled (except as provided in n. 11 for those who are "impeded"), the indulgence gained will be only partial.

8. The three conditions may be fulfilled several days before or after the prescribed work has been performed. However, it is appropriate that communion be received and the prayers for the Pope's intention be said on the same day the work is performed.

9. One sacramental confession suffices to gain several plenary indulgences. But for each plenary indulgence communion must be received and prayers for the Pope's intentions must be said.

10. One Our Father and one Hail Mary fully satisfy the condition of praying for the Pope's intentions; nevertheless, if a person wishes to substitute some other prayer according to his own piety and devotion towards the Pope he is free to do so.

According to these norms, a Catholic who watched or listened to the Pope's Christmas benediction would receive a plenary indulgence, but he could receive only one that day unless he was dying, in which case he could receive more than one. He also had to receive communion, make confession, and pray for the Pope's intentions of that day to get the plenary indulgence. If he did not meet these conditions, then the plenary indulgence became a partial indulgence.

Now if he were not able to perform these conditions on the same day, he could have performed them several days before or after and that would suffice, although communion and prayer for the Pope's intentions should be performed on the day itself. However, a confession is not necessary for each plenary indulgence because one confession is sufficient for several plenary indulgences, but communion and prayers for the Pope's intentions are necessary for each individual indulgence. One Our Father and one Hail Mary will satisfy the requirement of prayer for the Pope's intentions, or he can substitute a prayer of his own.

Friends, these are just ten out of twenty, and most Roman Catholics have no idea that such things are required. This is all a figment of man's imagination and nothing of the sort can be found anywhere in the pages of God's Word.

Tradition in the Roman Catholic Church

Tradition plays a very important role in the belief and practices of the Roman Catholic Church. For Roman Catholics there is great comfort to be found in the idea that a particular belief or practice "has always been" believed or practiced by their church. This is a major reason why non-Catholics have such difficulty understanding how Catholics can believe and practice things that are obviously not found in the Bible. Under the Roman Catholic system, Bible authority is not absolutely necessary. The Church teaches it, believes it, and practices it; therefore, it is true. While a Roman Catholic, I could not understand why non-Catholics were always bringing up the Bible and trying to disprove my beliefs by it. Certainly the Bible was important, but to my mind it did not present all the truth necessary. To grasp all the truth, one had to accept both the Bible and Roman Catholic tradition. I believed that the leaders of the church knew what was best, that they had always known what was best, and when something new was defined and added to the tradition, then that was the truth, plain and simple. Further study has shown me that tradition is not so clear-cut and obvious; actually, it is rather obscure. And the process whereby something becomes defined as a belief and practice of the Roman Catholic tradition is difficult to grasp.

What Is Tradition?

Trying to define "tradition" as it applies to the Roman Catholic Church is not as easy as it may seem. It is not a matter of merely looking in a book of Catholic beliefs and finding a definition. I looked in five different such books and found five different definitions. That should tell us something right there. But the clearest definition I found, as well as one that encompasses the basics from the others, is from the book *The Roman Catholic Church* by John L. McKenzie, S.J., where he states:

> Tradition can be viewed as channel and as content, to use a modern phrase. As content, it is a body of doctrine. . . .Tradition as channel thus becomes the teaching authority, the only authentic spokesman of Roman Catholic belief. Tradition can therefore be called living, for at any given moment it exists in the teaching authority (212).

So tradition includes not only the body of belief and practice unique to Roman Catholicism, but also the teaching authority of the church itself at any given time, thus enabling it to define further traditions.

The whole idea of tradition as it is now found in the Roman Catholic Church was not defined until 1546 by the Council of Trent, and then it was done to counter the reformers of the Protestant Reformation who demanded scriptural authority for religious practices. The following quote from *A Catholic Commentary on Holy Scripture* by Bernard Orchard shows the motivation behind the Council's decree:

> Through Luther, although Calvin seems to have been the first to announce Monobiblicism clearly, the Bible became the arm of the Protestant revolt. A dumb and difficult book was substituted for the living voice of the Church, in order that each one should be able to make for himself the religion which suited his feelings. And the Bible open before every literate man and woman to interpret for themselves was the attractive bait to win adherents (11).

Feeling the need to counteract the demand for Bible authority, we are told in *The Question Box* by Rev. Bertrand L. Conway, that the Council decreed:

> Seeing clearly that this truth and discipline are contained in the written books and the unwritten traditions which, received by the Apostles from the mouth of Christ Himself, or from the Apostles themselves, the Holy Ghost dictating, have come down even unto us, transmitted as it were from hand to hand, following the example of the orthodox Fathers, receives and venerates, with an equal affection of piety, all the books of the Old and New Testaments . . . and also the said traditions . . . preserved in the Catholic Church by a continuous succession (78).

You may have noticed in the decree by the Council of Trent that those traditions, which they venerate equally with the Old and New Testaments, are *preserved in the Catholic Church by a continuous succession.* That is very important. In *The Roman Catholic Church* we are told that in Roman Catholicism, "no proposition can be declared an article of faith unless perpetual belief in the church can be affirmed of it" (212). Because of this, when the Roman

Catholic teaching authority defines a new tradition as an article of faith, they teach that they are merely defining something that has always been believed by the Church. The devout Roman Catholic takes great comfort from that. I know that I did. How surprised I was to discover that when solid evidence of "perpetual belief" is lacking, the Roman Catholic authorities merely fabricate it. Let me give you a few noteworthy examples.

Again from the book, *The Roman Catholic Church,* we find:

> In the definition of the Mariological dogmas of the Immaculate Conception and the Assumption, it was evident that literary evidence of these beliefs was lacking from the earliest centuries. The Roman Church concluded from the literary evidence in which the beliefs are found that the beliefs were as old, at least in an implicit form, as the church itself, and thus was enabled to declare that these articles had always been believed in the church. The Roman Church, however, does not depend solely on literary and historical evidence; it depends on its own consciousness of its belief. . . .In the two dogmas mentioned, it was the consciousness of perpetual beliefs which are in harmony with these dogmas and which are themselves confirmed by these dogmas (212).

Consider this quote. As far as the Immaculate Conception and the Assumption of Mary are concerned, the Roman Catholic Church admits that there is no evidence from the earliest centuries of the church that indicates the early Christians, guided by the apostles and those who had known the apostles, believed in them. So they moved into literature from later centuries, and there they believe that they found these dogmas at least implied. So they moved forward on the assumption that these later century Catholics must have gotten their ideas from someplace, so that proves that the Church always believed in these two dogmas. They then defined the dogmas, and their definition of them acts as final proof that the church "perpetually believed" in them. In other words, essentially what the Church says is, "We believe it now; we wouldn't make a mistake. So that means the Church has always believed it"—despite the fact that there is no evidence from the earliest centuries that they did. You can judge such reasoning for yourself.

The Process

What is the process whereby a tradition becomes defined and part of Roman Catholic teaching and dogma? The Roman Catholic answer demonstrates how far we must go to attempt to prove something that is not contained in God's Word. In truth, there is no set process or formula accepted and recognized by all Roman Catholic theologians. John L. McKenzie, with surprising candor, states the following in *The Roman Catholic Church*:

Whatever be the process, it cannot be a process of deduction. Thomas Aquinas, by what he thought flawless logic, proved that Mary could not have been immaculately conceived; even the prince of theologians had his blind spots. Duns Scotus, by an argument, which does not so much defy logic as ignore it, was convinced that she was. The Roman church does not conceive that it arrives at such beliefs by logic. . . .Regarding both the Immaculate Conception and the Assumption, the Roman Church experienced a constant surging in itself toward the affirmation of these dogmas. At the risk of hypostatizing the institution, one can say that this surging, which went on for centuries before the declarations, gave the Roman Church a kind of inner compulsion to declare itself.

There you have it. Tradition, which is held with an equal degree of pious affection as is the Bible by the Roman Catholic Church, is arrived at, not by logic and a reasonable consideration of the evidence, but by a constant surging within the Church itself to believe something. That is the same as saying that for a long time the church wanted to believe something, we now believe it; therefore, it must be true. Also, if we now believe it, that proves that the church always believed it.

For those of us who believe in the need for Bible authority for all that we do in the realm of religion, that kind of reasoning and teaching is hard to accept. What kind of attitude permits the elevation of manmade traditions to the level of the authority of God's Word, which Word tells us that it is the complete and total, all-sufficient, final revelation of God?

Tradition Versus the Bible

The first sentence in the article entitled "Bible" from *The Catholic Reference Encyclopedia* is, "The collection of sacred Books, written under the inspiration of the Holy Spirit and recognized as such by the Church" (I: 182). That sounds really good. But if someone looks at that definition and says that the Scriptures are sacred books, "God-breathed" since they were written under the inspiration of the Holy Spirit, and must then be authoritative, perhaps even the sole source of authority, then the true Roman Catholic attitude toward the Scriptures will surface. They hold that the Bible was not even intended to be written, certainly not intended to be circulated, nor was it intended to be gathered into one book. They hold that it cannot be understood by the common man and thus is not a safe method for understanding God's Will for man, nor does it contain all truth. In fact, they call it a dead letter. How does all of this compare with what that Book, which they call sacred and inspired by the Holy Spirit, actually has to say?

Was the Bible Intended to be Written?

Is it true that the Bible was not intended to be written? From *The Question Box*, 1913 Edition, we read, "Is it not strange that if Christianity were to be learned from the Bible only, that Christ Himself never wrote a line or commanded his apostles to write; for their divine commission was not to write but to preach the gospel" (70). From the *Catholic Encyclopedia* we are told, "Christ gave his disciples no command to write, but only to teach" (V: 767).

My response to this is, "You do err, not knowing the scriptures nor the power of God" (Matt. 22:29). In 1 Corinthians 14:37 Paul wrote, "If any man think himself to be a prophet, or spiritual, let him acknowledge that the things that I write unto you are the commandments of the Lord." Paul was an Apostle, called by the grace of God to that work. Was he violating his commission to "only teach" by writing down the "commandments of the Lord"?

In Revelation 1:18-19 we find, "I am he that liveth and was dead; and, behold, I am alive forevermore, Amen: and have the keys of hell and of death. Write the things which thou hast seen, and the things which are, and the things which shall be hereafter." That is Jesus Christ, commissioning the Apostle John, to write the book of Revelation. Thus, in their assertion that the Bible was never intended to be written and that Christ never commanded His Apostles to write, the Roman Catholic authorities are just plain wrong.

Was the Bible Intended to be Circulated?

Are the Roman Catholic authorities correct when they say that the Scriptures were not intended to be circulated and that the Apostles had no idea that it would all eventually be gathered into one volume? Here are some assertions that the Catholics make. From *The Faith of Our Fathers* we find, "The Apostles are never reported to have circulated a single volume of the Holy Scripture, but 'they going forth, preaching everywhere, the Lord co-operating with them'" (66).

In light of that statement, how do they explain just one of several statements along this line that Paul made? He wrote, "And when this epistle is read among you, cause that it be read also in the church of the Laodiceans; and that ye likewise read the epistle from Laodicea" (Col. 4:16). Does this not sound like a command to circulate a letter?

From the *Campaigners for Christ Handbook,* we find, "There is in them no evidence whatever to suggest that it was the expectation of the writers that what they had written would one day be gathered together to become a part of the New Testament" (167). Is that correct? Do we not find a note of expectation in the words of the Apostle Paul in his discussion of spiritual gifts found in 1 Corinthians 12, 13, and 14?

In 1 Corinthians 13:8 Paul speaks of a time when miraculous spiritual gifts would fail, cease, and vanish away. In verses 9-10 he writes, "For we know in part, and we prophesy in part. But when that which is perfect is come, then that which is in part shall be done away." Is it not clear that Paul expected something that was "perfect" and that did not exist at that time to come? And is it not equally clear that he expected something that was in part at that time to be done away? Well, my friends, the New Testament is "that which is perfect." It is called "the perfect Law of liberty" in James 1:25. That which is was in part and done away with at the arrival of the complete New Testament was the partial revelation that they had at the time of Paul's writing. There is every reason to believe that the New Testament writers expected it to all come together and comprise the perfect, or complete, Will of God.

Is the Bible Understandable?

Is it true that the Bible is not understandable by the common man, as the Roman Catholic authorities assert? In *The Faith of Our Fathers* we find, "Second—A competent religious guide must be clear and intelligible to all, so that everyone may fully understand the true meaning of the instructions it contains. Is the Bible a book intelligible to all? Far from it; it is full of obscurities and difficulties not only for the illiterate, but even for the learned" (70).

> **"Is the Bible a book intelligible to all? Far from it; it is full of obscurities and difficulties not only for the illiterate, but even for the learned."**

In 2 Corinthians 1:13 Paul wrote, "For we write none other things unto you, than what ye read and acknowledge; and I trust ye shall acknowledge even to the end." Perhaps I should give that verse from a Catholic version. The Confraternity Version renders it, "For we write nothing to you that you do not read and understand. Indeed, I hope you will always understand."

In Ephesians 3:2-4 Paul wrote, "If ye have heard of the dispensation of the grace of God which is given to me to you-ward: How that by revelation he made known unto me the mystery (as I wrote afore in few words, Whereby, when ye read, ye may understand my knowledge in the mystery of Christ)." Certainly Paul believed that what he wrote could be understood by the common man. Again, the Roman Catholic authorities are wrong.

Does the Bible Contain All Truth Necessary?

Is it true that the Bible is not a safe method to find out what the will of the Lord is, and is it true that it does not contain all of the truth necessary, as the Roman Catholic Church teaches? From *The Question Box* we find, "The very nature of the Bible ought to prove to any thinking man the impossibility of its being the one safe method to find out what the Saviour taught" (67). From *The Faith of Our Fathers* comes this statement, "Now the Scriptures alone do not contain all the truths which a Christian is bound to believe, nor do they explicitly enjoin all the duties which he is obliged to practice" (72).

That is what the Catholic Church says. What does the Bible say? In 2 Timothy 3:16-17 we find, "All scripture is given by the inspiration of God, and is profitable for doctrine, for reproof, for correction, for instruction in righteousness. That the man of God may be perfect, thoroughly furnished unto all good works." 2 Peter 1:3 says, "According as his divine power hath given unto us all things that pertain unto life and godliness, through the knowledge of him that hath called us to glory and virtue."

Well, if the Scriptures are fit to thoroughly furnish an individual unto all good works, able to make him complete; and if they contain all things that pertain unto life and godliness, we must ask—what else is there?

Friends, God has revealed unto us His Will, and it is not contained in the traditions, commands, and doctrines of men. In fact, Jesus said, "This people draweth nigh unto me with their mouth, and honoreth me with their lips; but their heart is far from me. But in vain they do worship Me, teaching for doctrines the commandments of men" (Matt. 15:8-9). God's Will is contained in the pages of His Word, the Bible. For us today, His Will is specifically revealed in the New Testament.

Syllabus of Errors

During my years as a Roman Catholic there were occasional times when I heard mention of a document known as the *Syllabus of Errors*. Each time I heard the subject, it was brought up by non-Catholic friends and acquaintances. Not once did I hear about it from those people who had the responsibility of instructing me in the Catholic faith, the priests and other religious leaders. Upon investigation of this document I now understand why Catholic authorities in America have very little to say about it.

According to the *Catholic Encyclopedia*, the official title of this document is, "A syllabus containing the most important errors of our time which have been condemned by our Holy Father Pius IX in allocutions, at consistories, in encyclicals and other apostolic letters" (854). It has been shortened to simply *The Syllabus of Errors* and can be found in *The Sources of Catholic Dogma* by Henry Denzinger. Because of the method used in writing the document, it is sometimes difficult to understand. The errors are simply presented. In order to understand the positions held by the Roman Catholic Church, the reader must personally insert the words "It is not true that" before each of the statements. In all, there are eighty Errors set forth in the *Syllabus*. We are simply going to present eighteen of them with very little comment. All will be able to see that the Errors speak for themselves. To simplify for the reader, I will supply the words, "It is not true that" in parentheses before each Error.

Eighteen Errors

15. (It is not true that) "Every man is free to embrace and profess that which he, led by the light of reason, thinks to be true religion."

17. (It is not true that) "We must have at least good hope concerning the eternal salvation of all those who in no wise are in the true Church of Christ."

18. (It is not true that) "Protestantism is nothing else than a different form of the same true Christian religion, in which it is possible to serve God as well as in the Catholic Church."

21. (It is not true that) "The Church does not have the power of defining dogmatically that the religion of the Catholic Church is the only true religion."

24. (It is not true that) "The Church does not have the power of using force, nor does it have any temporal power, direct or indirect."

37. (It is not true that) "National churches can be established which are exempt and completely separated from the authority of the Roman Pontiff."

42. (It is not true that) "In a conflict between the laws of both powers, the civil law prevails."

45. (It is not true that) "The entire government of the public schools in which the youth of any Christian state is instructed, episcopal seminaries being excepted for some reason, can and should be assigned to the civil authority; and assigned in such a way, indeed, that for no other authority is the right recognized to interfere in the discipline of the schools, in the system of studies, in the conferring of decrees, in the choice or approval of teachers."

48. (It is not true that) "Catholic men can approve that method of instructing youth which has been divorced from Catholic Faith and the power of the Church, and which regards only, or at least primarily, the natural sciences and the purposes of social life on earth alone."

54. (It is not true that) "Kings and princes are not only exempt from the jurisdiction of the Church, but they also are superior to the Church in deciding questions of jurisdiction"

55. (It is not true that) "The Church is to be separated from the state, and the state from the Church."

57. (It is not true that) "The science of philosophy and of morals, likewise the civil laws, can and should ignore divine and ecclesiastical authority."

63. (It is not true that) "It is lawful to withhold obedience to legitimate rulers, indeed even to rebel."

67. (It is not true that) "By natural law the bond of matrimony is not indissoluble, and in various cases divorce, properly so-called, can be sanctioned by civil authority."

73. (It is not true that) "A true marriage can exist between Christians by virtue of a purely civil contract; and it is false to assert that the contract of marriage between Christians is always a sacrament; or that there is no contract if the sacrament is excluded."

77. (It is not true that) "In this age of ours it is no longer expedient that the Catholic religion should be the only religion of the state, to the exclusion of all other cults whatsoever."

78. (It is not true that) "Hence in certain regions of Catholic name, it has been laudably sanctioned by law that men immigrating there be allowed to have public exercises of any form of worship of their own."

80. (It is not true that) "The Roman Pontiff can and should reconcile and adapt himself to progress, liberalism, and the modern civilization" (437-442).

There we have eighteen of the eighty theses that make up the *Syllabus of Errors*. I believe that the things they teach are shocking. Bear in mind that this was issued in 1864 by the same Pope who would officially decree Papal Infallibility just six years later.

Outdated and Non-Applicable

My first reaction upon reading the *Syllabus* was, "That was over 100 years ago—they don't believe that anymore." My first reaction was wrong. Today the *Syllabus of Errors* is part of the ordination vows of every Roman Catholic priest. He takes an oath that he believes, and will defend, the eighty articles contained therein (*Roman Catholicism*, 26). Not one single part of it has been repudiated, and how could it? Pius IX, the very pope who decreed Papal Infallibility, is the one from whom these condemnations were taken.

Even more to the point is the statement made in the *Catholic Encyclopedia*, "Nevertheless, the syllabus must be accepted by all Catholics, since it comes from the Pope as universal teacher and judge, according to the official communication from Cardinal Antonelli accompanying it. Its contents cannot be challenged by Catholics, and they are to give assent to it, holding the opposite of the condemned propositions" (855).

Why is it that even though this is official Roman Catholic belief, American Roman Catholics are not taught it? In countries that are predominantly Catholic, the *Syllabus* is not only believed, it is practiced. As late as 1967, in the Religious Liberty Act passed by the Spanish Parliament, these are some of the laws and regulations governing non-Catholics. Protestants were not permitted to: establish a Protestant church without a license; be elected to any public office; establish a Protestant school; establish a seminary; publish or distribute religious literature without a license; be married in a Protestant (non-Catholic) wedding service (Protestants could only be married in a civil ceremony); engage in home evangelism; or bury their dead in public cemeteries (*Roman Catholicism*, 430-431). So yes, the *Syllabus of Errors* is believed and it is practiced today, in modern times, in countries that are predominantly Catholic.

Religious Toleration?

We are seeing a lot about various Protestant denominations engaging in dialogues with the Roman Catholic Church lately. The purpose of those talks is to bring these denominations under the umbrella of Rome while allowing them to retain certain of their distinctive rights and practices. As Father Christopher Phillips, the fifth married former Episcopal priest to be ordained a Catholic priest, says, "I believe this is the shape of ecumenism to come. Other denominations will be in communion with Rome but retain what is good about their devotions. This is real ecumenism" (*Catholic Telegraph* [August 19, 1983], 9).

The key to understanding what is taking place is in realizing that these denominations must be "in communion with Rome," under the authority of the Pope and answerable to him. But what about those denominations that refuse "communion with Rome"? How does Rome "officially" feel about those bodies, and what would her attitude be toward them if Catholics were in a majority in this country?

In *Christian Principles and National Problems* by Ostheimer and Delaney (as quoted from *Roman Catholicism* by Loraine Boettner), which bears the Imprimatur of the late Cardinal Spellman, we read:

> The non-Catholic and the non-baptized should be permitted to carry on their own form of worship as long as there would be no danger of scandal or perversion of the faithful. In a country where the majority are Catholics, the practice of Protestantism or paganism by an inconspicuous minority would be neither a source of scandal nor perversion to the adherents of the true faith (99).

In other words, in a country where Catholicism is in the majority, Protestant groups would be permitted to practice their religion as long as they remained, "an inconspicuous minority."

In *Catholic Principles of Politics* by John A. Ryan and Frances J. Boland, a much-used seminary text with the Imprimatur of Cardinal Spellman, we find:

Suppose that the constitutional obstacles to proscription of non-Catholics have been legitimately removed and they themselves have become *numerically insignificant*. What then would be the proper course of action for a Catholic State? Apparently, the latter State could logically tolerate only such religious activities as were confined to the members of the dissenting group. It could not permit them to carry on general propaganda nor accord their organization certain privileges that had formerly been extended to all religious corporations, for example, exemption from taxation (320).

That is a rather frightening prospect, even for most American Roman Catholics. Unfortunately, most American Roman Catholics do not know that this is the position of their church. I know I didn't.

The Saints

The saints have ever been, are, and ever will be the greatest benefactors of society, and perfect models for every class and profession, for every state and condition of life, from the simple and uncultured peasant to the master of science and letters, from the humble artisan to the commander of armies, from the father of a family to the ruler of peoples and nations, from simple maidens and matrons of the domestic hearth to queens and empresses.

So read the words of Pope Pius XI in *Divinus Illius Magistri*, December 31, 1929. They aptly describe the view taken by the Roman Catholic Church toward its saints. Indeed, the Roman Church believes that the saints are its finest product, the product that most authenticates it (*The Roman Catholic Church,* John L. McKenzie, S.J., 227).

What is the Roman Catholic version of a saint? Strictly speaking, a saint is an individual who has been canonized. That means that the title of saint is awarded to a deceased person after he or she has passed through a long legal process. This process is called canonization. Canonization involves a thorough investigation of the life and papers of the individual under investigation. As part of the process, there is one official of the church, officially called the "promoter of the faith" (but popularly referred to as "the devil's advocate"), whose job it is to seek to discover flaws in the candidate for sainthood. The Roman Church does not expect its saints to be free of flaws totally, but it does require that they be free of what the church terms "non-heroic" flaws. This part of the process involves human approval. Divine approval of the candidate is said to be found in miracles worked through the intercession of the individual in question. These miracles constitute an important part of the process.

Generally speaking, a candidate for sainthood must pass through several stages. The first step in the long line toward approval is approval of his "cult." If from there the examination proceeds well, he is declared to be "venerable." If all continues to go well, and at this point we are talking about miracles, then the candidate is beatified, meaning he is given the title of "blessed." If even more miracles can be produced from his or her life, the candidate moves on to canonization. In a very moving ceremony the individual is canonized using this seventeenth or eighteen century formula we find in *The Book of Catholic Quotations*, 1956, Imprimatur—Francis Cardinal Spellman:

> In honor of the holy and undivided Trinity, for the exaltation of the Catholic faith and the growth of the Catholic religion, by the authority of our Lord Jesus Christ, of the blessed Apostles Peter and Paul, and by our own, after mature deliberation, after offering many prayers to God, after having conferred with our venerable brethren, the Cardinals of the Holy Roman Church, and with the Patriarchs and Bishops present in Rome, we declare that the blessed _____ is a Saint and we inscribe his/her name in the list of Saints, in the name of the Father, and of the Son and of the Holy Ghost. Amen.

As a child, I prayed to certain saints, secure and confident that they were in heaven listening to me, watching over me, caring for me.

The Roman Catholic authorities take great care throughout this process, and they had better because they teach infallibility in the canonization of the saints. Some uninformed critics have said that sainthood can be bought; however, my research does not substantiate such a charge. In his book, *The Roman Catholic Church*, McKenzie addresses this issue directly. He writes, "Among the things that the Roman Church at its worst has never relaxed are its standards of canonization. It is simply not true and never has been true that it can be bought; bribery may hasten the process, but it cannot insure it. The Roman Church does not apologize for any of its saints."

This procedure was established, or formalized, by Pope Benedict XIV (1740-1758). While there have been special cases, this process normally cannot be initiated until fifty years after the death of the candidate, and there are other intervals of time involved within the process itself.

As a child, I prayed to certain saints, secure and confident that they were in heaven listening to me, watching over me, caring for me. The particular saint to whom most of my prayers and thoughts were directed was Gregory the Great, my patron saint. I remember taking cupcakes or suckers to school on his feast day. I remember reading about him, learning about him, trusting in the fact that he was my patron saint. It was a rude awakening indeed to learn that the Catholic veneration of saints was not true. Even more difficult to accept was the knowledge that the Roman Catholic authorities, those whom I trusted so implicitly with my spiritual welfare, knew it was not true yet allowed me to believe that it was. Is this the "sour grapes" of a disgruntled ex-Catholic? Let's let a Jesuit priest tell us and you can decide for yourselves.

Again from the book, *The Roman Catholic Church* by John L. McKenzie, S.J., published in 1969 and bearing the Imprimatur of Joseph P. O'Brien, S.T.D., Vicar General, Archdiocese of New York, we read:

> Before the rules of Benedict XIV, the procedure was much more relaxed, and in earlier centuries canonization sometimes occurred by popular acclamation. The early casual practices resulted in a few embarrassments: nonexistent saints like Philomena and George (a Christian reincarnation of the Marduk-Tiamat, Baal-Mot, and Perseus-Andromeda myths), and John Nepomuk, who conflated more than one person. Yet in spite of these embarrassments the Roman Church claims infallibility in the canonization of saints—more correctly, it permits its theologians to teach that it is infallible. In such cases, the infallibility is seen to relate to the quality of the heroism proposed for veneration rather than to the historical reality of the person (228).

Such a statement in an authorized Roman Catholic book makes me wonder just who or what I was venerating as a child. Infallibility must be retroactive or it is meaningless. The Roman Church claims infallibility in the canonization of saints yet in the same paragraph admits mistakes in their canonizations. Mistakes necessarily rule out infallibility. To cover the mistakes, they claim infallibility in "the quality of the heroism" proposed for veneration rather than in the reality of the person. Am I to believe, then, that I was praying to a quality? If they were wrong in these cases, how can their claim of infallibility be trusted in any other? They believed the individuals mentioned were historical people, canonized them, and claimed infallibility in doing so. They found out that they were wrong, so they adjusted the infallibility to cover the supposed qualities that were to be found in the non-existent person. Then to top it off, they allow their theologians to tell us that they are infallible. How in the world can anybody, once they know such a thing, continue to believe the statements of those who are responsible?

Statues, Relics, and Images in the Catholic Church

If a visitor walks into practically any large urban Roman Catholic Church building, he or she will see essentially the same things. Along both of the side walls there will be either pictures, statues, or symbols, fourteen in all, representing the Stations of the Cross. Toward the front of the building there will be a statue of Mary with rows of votive lights placed before her. On the other side, there will probably be a statue of the patron saint of that particular church, with another set of votive lights to be lit by the parishioners. Over the main altar, or very near it, will be a large crucifix. Most of the time there will be a statue of Jesus hanging on it. Scattered around the building there may be other statues and pictures of various Catholic saints. Considered purely from a human standpoint, a visit to a Roman Catholic Church building can be a most impressive sight. To a Roman Catholic, there is a certain amount of pride involved over the beauty of their building and a certain amount of comfort that comes from being surrounded by all of these familiar images.

Most Roman Catholics, as well as most visitors, simply accept the statues and images with little thought about where they came from or why they are there in the first place. Few realize that these statues and images were one of the main reasons that the Eastern Orthodox Church broke away from Roman Catholicism in A.D. 1054. To this very day Eastern Orthodox Churches are free of such images. So where did they come from? Did the early church and the apostles use them? Why are they in use in Roman Catholicism today? These are important questions that need to be answered.

How Did They Come To Be Used?

In the book, *What the Church Teaches* by J.D. Conway, and bearing the Imprimatur of Ralph L. Hayes, a questioner asks, "On what basis, then, does your Church permit kneeling before statues and for that matter, how can you even make and possess them?" This is a very good question, and Conway's answer is most enlightening. He writes:

> And now about those statues! We won't single them out, but rather group them with pictures, mosaics, carvings, and icons, under the general name of *images*. We have them in our churches *because we like them and have always been accustomed to them.* They are beautiful and decorative; or at least we intend them to be so, even though they often fail to match this purpose. They add color and warmth; our churches would seem *cold and drab without them.* They often teach us bits of our religion, attract our attention to pious subjects, and aid our concentration.
>
> Above all, images are an old Christian custom, going back to the days of the catacombs. In spite of a few rough days with the Iconoclasts, our religious ancestors always made use of images, even as we do, without worrying about idolatry.

We have them in our churches because we like them and have always been accustomed to them.

The use of images may be an "old custom," but it has little to do with the church that was built by our Lord Jesus Christ in approximately A.D. 33. The first-century church was without images. It existed for over 100 years before worship in the catacombs became commonplace and the influence of the idolatrous world began to make its presence felt among the Christians.

In the fourth century, when official status was given to the Church through the efforts of Constantine, the Emperor of Rome, suddenly there was a large influx of pagans into the favored church of the state, and the opposition to the use of images began to be overcome. Many of the new converts simply transferred their old pagan practices into their new form of religion. Even Conway makes this point in *What the Church Teaches* when he writes, "It seems manifest that Christians simply adapted the art of pagan Rome to their religious needs" (218).

Early in the seventh century, Gregory the Great officially sanctioned the use of images in the churches. The very fact that an official sanction was deemed necessary evidences the fact that not all accepted it and that there was opposition. Gregory insisted that they not be worshipped, but his insistence did not stop the natural progression of action among the people. By the eighth century so many prayers were being offered to the statues and images and there was such an atmosphere of superstition surrounding their use that the Mohammedans taunted the Catholics for being "idol-worshippers."

In A.D. 726, Leo II, the Eastern Emperor, took steps to remedy the abuse of images in his dominion. He ordered all the pictures and images to be placed so high that it would be impossible for the worshippers to kiss them. Even that didn't stop the people from "worshipping" the images, so he took one step more and forbade the use of all images in the churches. Ecclesiastical sanction was given to his actions by a Council in Constantinople in 754. This controversy was called the "Iconoclastic Controversy." Iconoclastic means "breaking the images." Conway referred to "a few rough days with the Iconoclasts" and flippantly dismissed it, but he neglected to say that a Catholic Council sanctioned the removal of images as heathenish and heretical.

Thirty-three years later, in 787, another Council met, this time at Nicaea, and reversed the decree of the earlier council, sanctioning the worship of images in the churches. In *What the Church Teaches* Conway writes, "In this ecumenical council—the last one accepted by all five Patriarchs—the doctrine of the Church regarding images *was clearly defined and settled once and for all*" (219).

If this is true, why did the Council of Trent, in 1564, find it necessary to issue a decree concerning the use of images in the churches? The issue was not settled in 787 because during the Reformation others raised their voices in protest of the use of images in religion. The Council of Trent finally decreed, "The Holy Synod commands that images of Christ, of the Mother of God and of the other saints be kept in churches, and that due honor and reverence be paid to them, not because it is believed that there is any divinity in them, or that anything may be asked of them, but because the honor which is done to them is done to the prototypes they represent."

Today Roman Catholic Churches are filled with images of all kinds, but be not deceived. They are not there as a result of the teaching and practice of the first-century church. They have not been steadily accepted since the time of the catacombs, and they are not as harmless as they may appear to the average, well-educated American Roman Catholic.

God-Authorized or Dangerous Additions?

In Exodus 20:4-5 we find the second commandment, "Thou shalt not make unto thee any graven image, or any likeness of anything that is in heaven above, or that is in the earth beneath, or that is in the water under the earth:

Thou shalt not bow down thyself to them, nor serve them." Thus in the Old Testament we find a strict prohibition concerning the making of images of anything above, on, or below the earth and then bowing down before them.

In Acts 17:29, as Paul was making his address from Mars Hill in Athens, he said, "Forasmuch then as we are the offspring of God, we ought not to think that the Godhead is like unto gold, or silver, or stone, graven by art and man's device."

I believe that these passages, and many others like them, are applicable to a discussion of the use of images in Roman Catholicism.

The Official Catholic Position

The official Roman Catholic position concerning the use of idols was stated in this way by the Council of Trent, Session XXV:

> The images of Christ and the Virgin Mother of God, and of the other saints, are to be had and to be kept especially in churches, and due honor and veneration are to be given them: not that any divinity or virtue is believed to be in them, on account of which they are to be worshipped, or that anything is to be asked of them or that trust is to be reposed in images, as was done of old by the Gentiles, who placed their hope in idols; but because the honor which is shown them is referred to the prototypes which these images represent; in such wise that by the images which we kiss, and before which we uncover the head, and prostrate ourselves, we adore Christ, and we venerate the saints whose likeness they bear.

Officially the Roman Catholic Church denies that its members pray to statues, but states that they pray to the persons the statues represent. The Church denies that they attribute any power to the statues and other images, or that they place any trust in them at all, but rather they say they place their trust in God and in the intercessory powers of the saints represented by the images. All of this sounds reasonable to the educated adult Roman Catholic, but for those less educated or mature, the official distinction set forth by the Roman Catholic authorities is obscure, and often completely ignored; and in many instances promoted by Catholic officials. Let's notice a few examples.

"By Their Fruits Ye Shall Know Them"

J.D. Conway, in his book *What the Church Teaches*, sums up his section on images in the Catholic Church with these words:

> To sum it up . . . we kneel before these statues because we can pray better there. They remind us of our Lord, to whom our prayers are directed, of His Mother,

and His Saints, who inspire and help us. You have pictures of your husband and children around your home; we have images of the ones we love in church. They help to make our churches beautiful, for the glory of the Lord. *And they do no harm at all; we have no tendency to adore them.*

Let's see if in actual practice Conway's words ring true. Emmett McLoughlin was a former Franciscan priest and author of the book, *People's Padre.* In this book he gives this description of an event that he witnessed:

> In the Mission of San Xavier del Bac near Tucson are carried on the same superstitions that American tourists find repugnant in the national shrines of Mexico. Mexicans and Indians make pilgrimages from Tucson and other nearby communities, usually on foot. They crawl on their knees through the church to the ancient wooden reclining statue of St. Francis Xavier. The early Mexican custom was to make nude statues similar to our store-window mannequins; the people would then make clothes for these saints—simple garments for weekdays and elaborate gowns of gold and silver for Sundays and feast days. On the cloth robes of St. Francis Xavier the Arizona pilgrims pin their "votive" offerings—either gifts promised if a favor is granted or an advance gift showing good faith in bargaining with the saint. These offerings are tiny metal figures from one to two inches in length, sold by Mexican silversmiths. They are the figures of babies, arms, legs, hands, heads, or women's breasts. They indicate that the petitioner wants a baby, or has broken a leg or an arm, or has a mal—a disease.
>
> The Franciscan priests who care for this mission do nothing to discourage this hopeless practice. In fact, when St. Francis' robe is overburdened, the priests remove the offerings so that pilgrims can start in again. I have seen a priest stir up a barrel of these offerings with a broom handle (85).

The Catholic authorities may say what they will, but to the mind of an honest observer the distinction between the statue and the "Saint" it is supposed to represent is for all intents and purposes non-existent.

The Scapular

Another form of Roman Catholic imagery is the scapular. I wore one of these as a child. The scapular was invented in 1287 by Simon Stock, an English monk. He was said to have withdrawn into the woods where he lived a life of great austerity for twenty years. At the end of the twenty years, the Virgin Mary was said to appear before him, with thousands of angels, holding the scapular in her hand. This was to be taken as the sign of the Carmelite Order of which he was a member. The scapular consists of two pieces of material, approximately four inches square, worn next to the skin, suspended over the shoulders by cords both in the front and back.

What use did modern Roman Catholic authorities make of this form of imagery? Paul Blanshard writes in *American Freedom and Catholic Power* the following:

> I have before me as I write a four-page circular called the Scapular Militia is-sued by the Carmelite National Shrine of Our Lady of the Scapular, of 338 East 29th Street, New York. It bears the official Imprimatur of Archbishop (now Cardinal) Spellman, and it was issued at the height of the war of 1943. The slogan emblazoned on its cover is "A Scapular for Every Catholic Service Man," and it carries, underneath, a picture of Mary, Joseph, and St. Simon Stock, the specific guarantee in heavy capitals, **WHOSOEVER DIES CLOTHED IN THIS SCAPULAR SHALL NOT SUFFER ETERNAL FIRE** (215-216).

Included in the circular were these words:

> A Carmelite Father showed the present writer a letter from a classmate who was directly fired upon by four machine guns, from a distance of 700 or 800 meters for a period of fifteen minutes, and who wrote in a token of gratitude of Our Lady of the Scapular, saying simply, "And here I am."

It also promised, "Besides this a Scapular wearer can assure his liberation from Purgatory on the first Saturday after death." On an inside page this statement was found, "A Scapular is not a talisman. It is not a rabbit's foot. It is the sign of devotedness to the Blessed Virgin, just as the carrying of your Mother's picture in a fold of your wallet would be a sign of your devotedness to her."

Very little comment needs to be made about such a thing. The official posi-tion of the Roman Catholic Church says one thing about its use of imagery, but its actual practice is something else. Who has not read accounts of Ro-man Catholic images that are said to bleed or to weep? In Buffalo, New York, on December 8, 1947, a copy of the Fatima Statue was viewed by 200,000 people. During its journey to America, miracles were reported to have taken place along its path.

My prayer is that as Roman Catholics read this, they will not say, "Well, I don't view statues in that way" and then dismiss what has been documented. Undoubtedly many educated, mature Catholics make the distinction the Church claims to teach. Equally without doubt, however, is the fact that many, many other Catholics do not.

Images in Catholicism are not of God. He specifically condemned such things in the Old Testament, and the dangers involved with them are recognized in the New. They are of the mind of man and pagan in origin. Just the few examples of actual practice that we have cited demonstrate the fact that they are dangerous additions. I am reminded of the words of Paul, "Wherefore come out from among them, and be ye separate, saith the Lord, and touch not the unclean thing; and I will receive you" (2 Cor. 6:17).

Relics in the Catholic Church

What is a relic? According to *The New Baltimore Catechism* a relic is, "Something belonging to, or connected with Our Lord or the Saints, such as a portion of their bodies or a garment they wore" (III: 312). The Roman Catholic Church further classifies relics as first, second, and third class. A first-class relic would be a part of the body of the saint. A whole arm, or leg, or head, or heart would be a major (insignis) first-class relic. Parts of the saints' clothing or other personal effects would be a second-class relic. Things such as paper, cloth, and so on that the saints touched would be third-class relics.

The official Roman Catholic position concerning the use of relics can be found in *The New Baltimore Catechism #3* in the following questions and answers:

> **According to** *The New Baltimore Catechism* **a relic is, "Something belonging to, or connected with Our Lord or the Saints, such as a portion of their bodies or a garment they wore."**

219. Why do we honor relics? We honor relics because they are the bodies of the saints or objects connected with the saints or with Our Lord. The honor given to a relic does not stop at the sacred object itself but is directed to the person whose relic is venerated.

222. Do we honor Christ and the saints when we pray before the crucifix, relics, and sacred images? We honor Christ and the saints when we pray before the crucifix, relics, and sacred images because we honor the persons they represent; we adore Christ and venerate the saints.

223. Do we pray to the crucifix or to the images and relics of the saints? We do not pray to the crucifix or to the images and relics of the saints, but to the

persons they represent. In venerating relics, statues, and pictures of Our Lord and the saints we must not believe that any divine power resides in them as though they had the power of themselves to bestow favors. We place our trust in God and the intercessory power of the saints.

So once again we find the Roman Catholic Church using an inanimate object to represent our Lord or a dead Catholic saint. According to Catholic authorities these inanimate objects are not to be worshipped themselves; the worship or veneration goes to the people they represent. Nor are Catholics to believe that there is any power possessed by the relics themselves. In theory this may sound plausible, but even Roman Catholics will have to admit that in practice what is said and what is done are two different things.

How Are Relics Used?

One of the most interesting usages of relics in Roman Catholicism concerns the altars upon which Roman Catholic masses are offered. In *The New Code of Canon Law*, 1983, we read, "The ancient tradition of keeping the relics of martyrs and other saints under a fixed altar is to be preserved according to the norms given in liturgical books" (Canon 1237, #2). Just what that tradition in the liturgical books involves can be found in *The Beauties of the Catholic Church* by Rev. F. J. Shadler. In answer to the question, "Are relics of the saints put into all the altars even at present?" Shadler responds, "Yes: and the discipline of the Church in this respect is so strict that it is forbidden to celebrate Mass upon an altar in which there are no relics."

The Catholic Encyclopedia Dictionary states, "It is necessary for the valid consecration of an altar, whether fixed or portable, that it contain, sealed into the sepulcher, relics of at least one martyr."

One wonders why the Roman Catholic Church has such strict regulations concerning relics in their altars, if in fact the relics are not the objects of worship themselves and contain no powers in and of themselves. Why forbid the offering of a mass if a relic of a saint is not present at the altar?

Paul Blanshard makes another interesting point concerning relics in the altars in *American Freedom and Catholic Power* where he writes, "If fourteen thousand Catholic churches in the United States have an average of four altars each, this requirement calls for fifty-six thousand relics of martyrs in this country alone. New churches, of course, require new relics or portions of old ones" (218). Where do all of these relics come from and how can they possibly be authenticated? This is a question that Catholic authorities anticipate and here is how they answer it.

From *The Question Box* we read, "The Catholic Church has never declared that any particular relic is authentic, but she takes the greatest pains to see that no public honor is paid to any relic, unless she is reasonably convinced of its genuine character" (373). Does it make any sense to forbid the offering of a mass on an altar unless the altar contains a relic, and then to admit that they cannot say for certain whether or not the relic is authentic? Something does not ring true here.

Within the Roman Catholic Church there appears to be recognition of the fact that many of the better educated, more knowledgeable Roman Catholics will not fall for belief in relics, and that many of them view it as little more than superstition. Because of this the Roman Catholic Church does not impose compulsory belief in relics upon its members. Yet there are vast numbers of Roman Catholics who do believe in relics, who make pilgrimages to shrines containing them, and who spend vast amounts of money in the course of their veneration of relics. How, then, does the Roman Catholic Church handle these two different views? *The Catholic Encyclopedia Dictionary* says, "No Catholic is formally bound to the positive veneration of relics, *but is forbidden by the Council of Trent to say that such veneration ought not to be given.*" In other words, those Catholics who disagree with the whole system of relic veneration do not have to believe, but they have to keep their mouths shut and not speak out against it. For those who do believe, the Roman Catholic authorities are more than willing to provide them with as many relics as they can stand.

Some Examples

We have seen that the Roman Catholic Church has never declared that any particular relic is authentic. Maybe not, but she has come as close to doing so as she possibly can. There has been much written lately about the Shroud of Turin. It has received a great deal of publicity. However, for quite some time now the Roman Catholic Church has been presenting it as the real thing. Back in 1947, a large advertisement with a reproduction of a "photograph" of Jesus taken from the Shroud of Turin appeared in *The Catholic News* with this guaranty. Judge for yourselves if this "relic" was being presented as authentic:

> The negative from which this photograph was made lies in the Holy Shroud and was developed in the Tomb during the hours Our Lord lay there before

the Resurrection. The urea vapors emanating from the body acted on the aloes within the Shroud, creating the indissoluble pigment, aloetin, which was absorbed by the Shroud linen, thus forming the *True Image of Christ. . . .*The official Vatican Newspaper says: *"Twenty centuries ago the Apostles saw and kissed this same living Face."*

For just $2.00 you could get a picture of *The True Face of Christ from the Holy Shroud of Turin.*

The *Catholic Almanac* of 1948 says:

Isn't there something inherently wrong with admitting that there is no proof of authenticity, and then presenting these things as though they were authentic?

There are various relics of the *true cross* to be found principally in European cities: Brussels, Ghent, Rome, Venice, Ragusa, Paris, Limbourg, and Mt. Athos. The inscription placed above the cross is preserved in the Basilica of the Holy Cross of Jerusalem at Rome. The crown of thorns is kept at Paris. One of the nails was supposedly thrown into the Adriatic to calm a storm; another was made into a famous iron crown at Lombardy; another is in the Church of Notre Dame, Paris. The sponge is in Rome at the Basilica of St. John Lateran. The point of the lance is in Paris, the rest is in Rome. The tunic is in the Church of Argenteuil near Paris. A part of the winding sheet is in Turin. The linen with which Veronica wiped Christ's face is in Rome. Part of the pillar of the Scourging is in Rome, part in Jerusalem (250).

Isn't there something inherently wrong with admitting that there is no proof of authenticity, and then presenting these things as though they were authentic? Isn't there something inherently wrong with charging money for a picture of a "religious relic" when it cannot be said with certainty that the relic is actually the thing it is supposed to be? If these things are real, why allow some Catholics to refuse to believe in them and yet demand that they keep their mouths shut about their doubts? These things need to be considered.

The One True Church, According to Catholicism

Despite certain recent statements made by Catholic authorities that seemingly indicate a movement towards ecumenism, despite the much-publicized steps in that direction taken by the Second Vatican Council, the Roman Catholic Church has, does now, and will in the future, teach the doctrine of "The One True Church." The questions to be answered are: What does that doctrine mean? How did they arrive at it? By what logic do they sustain it? And what is the primary emphasis of the doctrine? To what do the Catholic authorities attach the greatest importance as far as "The One True Church" is concerned?

In *The New Code of Canon Law*, we find in Canons 204 and 205 the following:

204-1 The Christian faithful are those who, inasmuch as they have been incorporated in Christ through baptism, have been constituted as the people of God; for this reason, since they have become sharers in Christ's priestly, prophetic and royal office in their own manner, they are called to exercise the mission which God has entrusted to the Church to fulfill in the world, in accord with the condition proper to each one.

204-2 This Church, constituted and organized as a society in this world, subsists ("exists" or "lives"—*Webster's Dictionary*) in the Catholic Church, governed by the successor of Peter and the bishops in communion with him.

205 Those baptized are fully in communion with the Catholic Church on this earth who are joined with Christ in its visible structure by the bonds of profession of faith, of the sacraments and of ecclesiastical governance.

In order for baptized people to share in Christ's priestly, prophetic and royal office, in order for them to be joined with Christ in the Church, they must be members in full communion with the Catholic Church; because according to Canon Law, the Church, constituted and organized as a society in this world, lives or exists in the Catholic Church.

Further statements concerning the Catholic doctrine of "The One True Church" can be found in numerous places. We will quote from the book, *The Roman Catholic Church*, written by John L. McKenzie, S.J., while he was a professor of theology at the University of Notre Dame. Under the section entitled, "The One True Church," McKenzie writes:

> There always had to be a church and only one church. It was not conceivable that the church should break up into fragments. When division happened, that body which could most successfully assert its continuity with the church before division maintained itself as the one, holy, catholic, and apostolic church.

> It has been shown that the primacy of Rome began in the fourth century to develop the form which it finally achieved. The Roman primacy then became the test of unity; the one, holy, catholic, and apostolic church adds the word Roman to these titles, for it is that church which recognizes the Bishop of Rome as the bishop of bishops. It is his teaching and his obedience which authenticate the one true church: the Roman is the church which endures, which remains the one true church through all divisions (117).

As Long As It Applies, Use It. When It Doesn't, Don't.

In the quotes already given, we have shown a degree of the reasoning used by the Roman Catholic authorities to arrive at this doctrine of "The One True Church." Let's now show a degree of convoluted logic, or the use of a certain method of reasoning, until it no longer favors their ideas. Again from McKenzie's book, *The Roman Catholic Church*, we read:

> In the doctrine of the one true church, *there is an implicit appeal to the majority*. This is reflected in the scoffing question of Optatus addressed to the Donatists, whether they think the one true church is confined to an obscure region of the province of Africa. It is reflected in a quotation from Augustine, which John Henry Newman said influenced him deeply when he was thinking about his submission to Rome: 'Securus judicat orbis terrarum," which we may roughly paraphrase, "the judgment of the whole world is delivered free from pressure." Roman theology *has cherished this implicit appeal while at the same time it has rejected the implication that Roman Catholicism would cease to be the one true church if it should become a minority of the Christian body.* The one true church is and must remain the Church of Rome (118).

Think about what McKenzie has said. As long as the Catholic Church is in the majority, being in the majority acts as substantial proof that they are the one true church. If they cease to be in the majority, then the majority means nothing. Truly, what kind of reasoning is that? If I may, allow me to refer to the true authority, our Lord Jesus Christ, and let Him tell us what significance should be placed on the majority: "Enter ye in at the strait gate: for wide is the gate, and broad is the way, that leadeth to destruction, *and many there be which go in thereat*; Because strait is the gate, and narrow is the way, which leadeth unto life, *and few there be that find it*" (Matt. 7:3-14).

If you should happen to be a member of the Roman Catholic Church and have listened to, or taken comfort from, the implied appeal to the majority which the Catholic authorities have admittedly used, reject it. Jesus certainly did. Being in the majority proves nothing, particularly not the idea of being "The One True Church."

What is of the Greatest Importance to the Mind of Roman Authorities?

To answer this question, two words must be considered and defined. They are "schism" and "heresy." According to *The New Code of Canon Law*, we find in Canon 751:

> Heresy is the obstinate post-baptismal denial of some truth which must be believed with *divine* and catholic faith, or it is likewise an obstinate doubt concerning the same . . . schism is the refusal of *submission to the Roman Pontiff* or of communion with the members of the Church subject to him.

"In schism the identity of the church is really more imperiled than by heresy."

McKenzie, in his book *The Roman Catholic Church*, said, "The opposite of faith is heresy, the denial of an article of faith" (194). In the same book he says, "Schism of itself has nothing to do with belief; it is a refusal to recognize authority in a legitimate officer of the church" (117).

So, "heresy" is an obstinate denial or even an obstinate doubt of a *divine* article of faith. "Schism" is the refusal to submit to the Roman Pontiff or one of the other officials of the Catholic Church. Wouldn't you suppose that the most serious and dangerous of these two would be heresy, denying a divinely given truth, turning your back on the revealed Word of God? Not according to the Roman Catholic concept of what is important in "The One

True Church." Again McKenzie, under the section entitled "The One True Church" writes, "In schism the identity of the church is really more imperiled than by heresy" (117).

We are compelled to ask, what is the point? Is the church to teach the truth and guard the truth? Is it to be the "pillar and ground of the truth" as Paul told Timothy in 1 Timothy 3:15? Or is the most important thing having the people in subjection to a human being—having the people submissive to a man and his appointed officials over and above God's truth? The Catholic concept of "The One True Church" has as its very cornerstone, submission to the pope and other members of the Catholic hierarchy. That is the primary emphasis behind it.

The whole idea, which is being taught as strongly now by Catholic authorities as it used to be, simply does not hold water as far as the Catholic Church is concerned. What is more important—divine truth, or the power that comes from having millions of people in subjection to you?

The Council of Trent

As I look back on my years in the Catholic Church, one of the events that stands out in my mind was the convening of the Second Vatican Council. It took place when I was a young boy in the early years of my parochial school education, and it was exciting to think that the greatest minds and leaders of the Church were gathering in Rome to address the problems and issues confronting the Church. Even at such a tender age, it was comforting to think that with divine guidance these men were making decisions that would assure my spiritual welfare. The nuns took the opportunity to teach us of the importance of such ecumenical councils, telling us that they constituted one of the greatest guarantees of the Church's unity and integrity of doctrine. We were taught as the *Code of Canon Law* tells us in Canon 228, "An oecumenical council has supreme power over the entire church." As part of our instruction concerning general councils, great emphasis was placed upon the greatest of all such councils to date, "The Council of Trent."

As we begin our examination of the Council of Trent, let me give some examples of what Catholics are taught by their church concerning it. From the book, *Christianity and Civilization*, we find:

> The Council of Trent (1545-1563), meeting over nearly a twenty-year period, often interrupted by wars and politics, clarified the teaching of the Church on the issues raised and attacked by the Protestants. It published a catechism in which its stand was clearly defined. It reaffirmed that the Scriptures *and tradition* were the basis of the Catholic religion, and rejected private judgment by reserving to the Church the right to interpret the Bible. It denied the doctrine of justification by faith alone and insisted on the necessity of good works. Papal supremacy in the Church and the necessity of the seven sacraments were likewise reaffirmed by the Council.

To eliminate many of the abuses that had developed in the Church, *the Council of Trent promulgated long overdue disciplinary statutes. . . .*Many of the financial abuses were likewise eliminated (284-285).

In the *Catholic Encyclopedia* we find:

The Council of Trent was the Church's answer to the Protestant Reformation. It delimited Catholic doctrine sharply from Protestant and eliminated the disastrous obscurity as to what was an essential element of the faith and what was merely a subject for theological controversy. . . . The reform decrees of the Council were a compromise between the radical Reformers' wishes and the curial tradition, not an ideal solution but a serviceable one. *Wherever implemented, they effected a renewal and strengthening of ecclesiastical life. The new Catholic piety and mysticism, the revival of scholastic theology, the emergence of positive theology, and the art and culture of the baroque age depend upon the Council of Trent or at least are inconceivable without it. It was no mere restoration of the Middle Ages; rather it brought so many new features to the countenance of the Church that with it a new era of Church history begins* (277).

The first most revealing fact about the Council of Trent is that it was not convened by Pope Paul III due to his own desire for reform, nor was it due to the demands of the Catholic hierarchy. It was convened because of pressure from the secular leaders of Europe, particularly from Emperor Charles V.

With statements such as these it is easy to see that the Catholic authorities present the Council of Trent as a "gem" in a long line of important and distinguished general councils. It was, after all, the Catholic answer to the Protestant Reformation. However, it is shocking to find that what the Catholic Church tells its members concerning this council, indeed what they tell the world, is false.

For the statements that will follow, I have used as my sources the following books: *American Culture & Catholic Schools* by Emmett McLoughlin, *History of Sacerdotal Celibacy in the Christian Church*, and various other works by Henry Charles Lea.

The first most revealing fact about the Council of Trent is that it was not convened by Pope Paul III due to his own desire for reform, nor was it due to the demands of the Catholic hierarchy. It was convened because of pressure from the secular leaders of Europe, particularly from Emperor Charles V.

A second vital point is the reason for the call of a council by the European leaders. It was not because of doctrinal reform or declaration—it was for a moral problem. The European leaders wanted *the abolition of celibacy and permission for the priests to marry.* The reason for such concern was that many of the clergy were either already married anyway or living in concubinage. Any number of readily available history books, in addition to the ones I have mentioned, will support these statements. You will not find them supported by Catholic writers, not even in the *Catholic Encyclopedia.*

Another interesting fact is that while the Council of Trent is generally dated from 1545-1563, it was actually ordered opened by Pope Paul III on May 17, 1537; however, no delegates came. *American Culture & Catholic Schools* says, "Still by May 1, 1538, no bishops or cardinals had presented themselves to show any interest in reforming the Church. (Luther had made his break in 1517, twenty-one years before.)" On November 22, 1542, Pope Paul III ordered the Council convened once again, but so few representatives came that it was suspended once again in July of 1543. Two years later it was convened again, formally opening on December 13, 1545, with a total of twenty-five delegates from all of the Catholic Church presuming to undertake the reform of the entire body. Again from *American Culture & Catholic Schools* we read:

> For fifteen months, this handful of ecclesiastics purported to represent the entire Church and, under the control of the Pope, expounded on dogma and dogmatics and completely ignored the purpose for which the Council had been forced upon them—the reform of the clergy, particularly through the ecclesiastical approval of their unions with the women of their choice through legitimized marriage (114).

In 1549, the Council was suspended again, only to be reconvened by Pope Julius III on May 1, 1551. On April 28, 1552, it broke up again. For ten more years, pressure from the common people, as well as their leaders, grew until Pope Pius IV again opened the Council on January 18, 1562. Many of the Catholic laity, as well as some devout local bishops and secular rulers, pleaded for reform, and the truth is that they got little or no cooperation from Rome for their efforts.

It is interesting as well that in 1560, two years before the Council was reconvened, Emperor Ferdinand I asked that it be called again with specific legislation permitting the marriage of the clergy. What the Council of Trent actually did was to restate many of the positions that had caused the problems in the first place. Concerning the problem of the unnatural state of celibacy and its attendant abuses, which had prompted the secular rulers to call for the Council in the first place, this is what the Council of Trent had to say in Session 24 on November 11, 1563:

> If any one saith that clerics constituted in sacred orders or regulars who have solemnly professed chastity are able to contract matrimony, and that being contracted it is valid notwithstanding the ecclesiastical law or vow; and that the contrary is nothing else than to condemn marriage; and that all who do not feel that they have the gift of chastity, even though they have made a vow thereof, may contract marriage; let him be anathema (Canon 9).

A valid question is this: Why, in all of the instructions I received as a parochial school student concerning the Council of Trent, and in all of the reading of Catholic works about it since that time, was no word mentioned of the true reason for the Council in the first place? Why is it that in a seven-page article in the *Catholic Encyclopedia* concerning the Council of Trent no mention is made of clerical immorality? Why are such things denied or ignored?

The truth is that in its two primary objectives (the reconciliation of "heretics" and the "purification" of the clergy), the Council of Trent was a dismal failure.

Mental Reservation

As a youngster growing up in the Roman Catholic Church, I would occasionally hear comments from non-Catholics about something called "Mental Reservation." Usually they were made by those who were anti-Catholic and who were accusing the Roman Catholic Church of allowing its members to lie. Since I did not fully understand what mental reservation was all about, my inclination was to disregard such comments as just further examples of Protestant prejudice. I was confident that no system of morality that was based upon the Word of God would permit such a thing, and to my mind, Catholicism was the only true system of morality that there was. My studies in recent years have demonstrated to me just how wrong I was.

What is Mental Reservation?

The only fair way to examine this subject is to allow the Catholic writers to tell us what mental reservation is and to illustrate how it can be used in everyday life. Are Catholics permitted to lie under certain circumstances? Read for yourself.

In the book, *The Question Box*, by Bertrand L. Conway of the Paulist Fathers, bearing the Imprimatur of Patrick Cardinal Hayes (Archbishop of New York at the time of publication), we find:

> Mental reservation is an act of the mind, which restricts the natural meaning that the spoken words appear to bear. If I give no outward clue to my mental limitation of the spoken phrase, either in the peculiar wording I use, or in the circumstances of person and of place, I am using a pure mental reservation, or, in plain English, a lie. If I do indicate externally my mental limitation according to the usages of language and of social custom, I am using a broad mental reservation, *which is always permissible and lawful* (432).

To further explain what mental reservation is we will present the following statement from *College Moral Theology*, a textbook for university usage by Anthony F. Alexander, a priest in the Department of Religion of John Carroll University. This book bears the Imprimatur of Samuel Cardinal Stritch, who was the Archbishop of Chicago at the time of publication in 1957. In this book we read:

> A person is permitted to use mental reservation when a just secret must not or need not be divulged to an unauthorized inquirer. In mental reservation the *deception* results because of the listener's unwarranted conclusion from misinterpreted premises. The speaker uses words which have several commonly accepted meanings. If the listener knew all the facts, he would have taken the same meaning as was in the speaker's mind. But the speaker has no duty to reveal them because the listener has no right to them. Notice that the speaker does not represent the premises as complete, and he does not draw the faulty conclusion for the listener. . . .*It is permissible to affirm legitimate mental reservation with an oath, for this circumstance does not change its intrinsic nature. If the speaker is under obligation to give information but hides it by mental reservation, he does not lie but may be the cause of injustice* (238).

"A few examples will illustrate our teaching. An importunate visitor, who has called repeatedly at my home, and borrowed money from me, which he never dreamed of repaying, is told by my intelligent servant, "My master is not at home." Do not the usages of modern society make it clear that I am not at home *TO HIM?*"

Now all of this is just obscure enough to sound somewhat reasonable to those who do not take the time to examine what is actually being said, or to consider how such a doctrine might be put into practice. Fortunately, we do not have to speculate about how this would be put into practice because Catholic writers have given us illustrations. Again we ask, "Are Catholics permitted to lie under certain circumstances?" Read for yourself.

Mental Reservation In Practice

From *The Question Box* we find:

A few examples will illustrate our teaching. An importunate visitor, who has called repeatedly at my home, and borrowed money from me, which he never dreamed of repaying, is told by my intelligent servant, "My master is not at home." Do not the usages of modern society make it clear that I am not at home *TO HIM?*

Cardinal Newman gives a good instance: "What news from France, my lord?" someone asked of a cabinet minister. "I do not know," he replied, "I have not read the papers." No private citizen has the right to expect a government official to disclose a government secret in the course of an ordinary conversation.

A priest may be asked in court—he has been asked—to divulge the divine secret of the confessional, and he answers rightly: "I do not know." He does not know *with a communicable knowledge*, and all the courts of the civilized world grant him the right to guard inviolate the sacred seal (433).

There you have it. According to "Mental Reservation," Catholics can indeed lie under certain circumstances. You can even have it said that you are not home when you are, just because you don't want to talk to someone. That is not my illustration; that is one of the illustrations used by a Catholic writer to illustrate their doctrine. Most of the Catholic laity do not know this and would be appalled if they did. Most of the good Catholic people know enough to know that a lie is a lie, and all of the theological ramblings about it won't change that fact.

Proverbs 12:22 says, "Lying lips are abomination to the Lord: but they that deal truly are his delight." The Catholic doctrine of "Mental Reservation" does not change the truth of God.

The New Code of Canon Law

On January 23, 1983, Pope John Paul II promulgated *The New Code of Canon Law* and declared that it would have "judicial binding force" from the first day of Advent, 1983 onward. This was the culmination of a great deal of work over an extended period of time and was eagerly awaited by the bishops of the Roman Catholic Church, as well as the rest of the clergy. The *Code* was called by Pope John Paul II, "the Church's principal legislative document founded on the juridical-legislative heritage of revelation and tradition" (*Code of Canon Law*, Apostolic Constitution, xiv). It contained 1,752 different canons and was sent out into the world with these words from Pope John Paul II:

> Trusting therefore in the help of divine grace, sustained by the authority of the blessed apostles Peter and Paul, with certain knowledge, in response to the wishes of the bishops of the whole world who have collaborated with me in a collegial spirit, and with the supreme authority with which I am vested, by means of this Constitution, to be valid forever in the future, I promulgate the present Code as it has been set in order and revised. I command that for the future it is to have the force of the law for the whole Latin Church, and I entrust it to the watchful care of all those concerned in order that it may be observed (xiv).

We will trace the development of this "law for the whole Latin Church."

The Roman Catholic Church has always felt a need to gather all of its laws into one book to facilitate knowledge and observance of them. This need led to the existence of a countless number of private collections of ecclesiastical laws, some of which were taken from the decrees of councils, Roman Pontiffs, and other lesser sources. Naturally, this led to a state of confusion as far as Ecclesiastical Law for the Roman Church was concerned. In the middle of the twelfth century, a monk by the name of Gratian undertook the putting together of this mass of laws into a single orderly document. It was called the Decretum Gratiani and constituted the first part of a most significant collection of laws of the Roman Church called the Corpus Iuris Canonici.

In the Preface to the Latin Edition of the *Code of Canon Law* we read:

> Besides the Decree of Gratian, in which the earlier norms were contained, the Corpus consists of the Liber Extra of Gregory IX, the Liber Sextus of Boniface VIII, the Clementinae, i.,e. the collection of Clement V promulgated by John XXII, to which are added the Extravagentes of the pope and the Extravagantes communes, decretals of various Roman pontiffs never gathered in an authentic collection (xvii).

> The Corpus Iuris Canonici is generally regarded as the classical law of the Catholic Church.

Laws that were set forth after the Corpus Iuris Canonici were not put into one collection, so once again the Roman Catholic Church found itself with an immense pile of separate ecclesiastical laws. Therefore, the bishops of the Roman Church began to ask for a single collection of laws. Pope Pius X undertook the task, and even though he did not complete it, this requested, "universal, exclusive, and authentic collection was promulgated on May 27, 1917 by his successor Benedict XV; it took effect on May 19, 1918" (*Code of Canon Law*, Preface, xviii).

This *Code of Canon Law*, the Pio-Benedictine Code, was welcome and widely effective for the Roman Catholic Church. However, times were changing, and in 1959 Pope John XXIII announced his decision to reform the *Code* of 1917. Pope John XXIII would not live to see the new *Code*. Vatican II would take place in 1962-1965, and Popes Paul VI and John Paul I would be called on to continue the reform. All of this work resulted in *The New Code of Canon Law* that we are discussing. Included in it are the latest laws of the Catholic Church, including those set forth in Vatican II.

We were told by Pope John Paul II that this *New Code* contained "the substantial newness of the Second Vatican Council." He told us, "*The New Code of Canon Law* appears at a moment when the bishops of the whole Church not only are asking for its promulgation, but are crying out for it insistently and almost with impatience" (*New Code of Canon Law*, Apostolic Const., xv).

Thus *The New Code of Canon Law* came forth as an eagerly awaited document, a document that would reform the old and contain the "substantial newness of the Second Vatican Council." One does not have to look very deeply into some of the authorized writings of Roman Catholic authors after Vatican II to realize that there was a feeling of expectation, almost anxiousness, among the clergy for this *New Code*. It would contain the changes brought about by Vatican II; it would breathe all of the new ecumenical spirit; it would relax some of the stringent censorship under which they labored. Well, the *New Code* came out. But was it new, different, and ecumenical, or was it the same old thing? Let's look at a few of the expectations voiced by Catholic authors and then look at the canons corresponding to them. You can judge for yourself.

Expectations

The publishing company of Holt, Rinehart and Winston published a *History of Religion* series. Included in that series was the book, *The Roman Catholic Church*, written by John L. McKenzie, S.J., a professor of theology at the University of Notre Dame. It was published in 1969 and bears the Nihil Obstat of Fall Higgins, O.F.M. Cap., Censor Librorum, and the Imprimatur of Joseph P. O'Brien, S.T.D., Vicar General, Archdiocese of New York. The intent of the book was to provide an in-depth look at the structure, worship, belief, and works of the Roman Catholic Church. In the introduction, McKenzie stated that the Roman Catholic Church stands at what may be the most critical point of its entire history. He wrote, "The Roman Catholic Church is passing into a crisis of authority and a crisis of faith." As he progressed in his writing he made mention of a number of practices and laws of Catholicism about which there was considerable controversy and concerning which change was anticipated. At times he anxiously looked forward to these changes. Bear in mind, this book was published after the Second Vatican Council but before the promulgation of *The New Code of Canon Law*.

The New Ecumenical Spirit—Marriage

In the section of his book, *The Roman Catholic Church*, entitled "The One True Church," McKenzie writes:

> The Roman Church interprets the ancient practice of denial of communion as signifying the denial of the Eucharist; it neither gives the Eucharist to Protestants nor receives it from them, since it does not admit that Protestants are capable of celebrating or of receiving the Eucharist. Its laws prohibit marriage between Catholics and Protestants; the laws permit dispensation, but demand that the ceremony be witnessed by a Catholic priest. It is only within the last

few years that the Roman Church has thought of abandoning its celebrated pledges that the children should be baptized and reared in Roman Catholicism. This version of the one true church is now under examination in Romanism; at this writing it is too early to predict what will emerge, but it seems safe to predict that the rigorous position which endured from the Council of Trent to the Second Vatican Council will not be reaffirmed (120).

Let's now see if Roman Catholicism is really changing its position as McKenzie predicted. From *The New Code of Canon Law*:

Without the express permission of the competent authority, marriage is forbidden between two baptized persons, one of whom was baptized in the Catholic Church or received into it after baptism and has not left it by a formal act, and the other of whom is a member of a church ecclesial community which is not in full communion with the Catholic Church (Canon 1124).

The local ordinary can grant this permission if there is a just and reasonable cause; he is not to grant it unless the following conditions have been fulfilled:

1. The Catholic party declares that he or she is prepared to remove dangers of falling away from the faith and makes a sincere promise to do all in his or her power to have all the children baptized and brought up in the Catholic Church.

2. The other party is to be informed at an appropriate time of these promises which the Catholic party has to make, so that it is clear that the other party is truly aware of the promise and obligation of the Catholic party (Canon 1125).

Before or after the canonical celebration held in accord with the norm of 1, it is forbidden to have another religious celebration of the same marriage to express or renew matrimonial consent; it is likewise forbidden to have a religious celebration in which a Catholic and a non-Catholic minister, assisting together but following their respective rituals, ask for the consent of the parties (Canon 1127).

My friend, the language may be a little different, but don't be fooled—it is the same old thing.

Anticipated Changes in Censorship—Did It Happen?

In the chapter of his book, *The Roman Catholic Church,* entitled "The Beliefs of the Roman Catholic Church," in the section, "The Teaching Office of the Church," McKenzie states:

A less defensible aspect of the teaching office is the supervision which the Roman Church has exercised over Catholic learning since the Protestant Reformation, especially over learning in which priests are engaged. Priests who write on any subject must submit their manuscripts to Episcopal authority for approval (CIC 1386). Lay scholars are under the same supervision for works on the Bible, theology, canon law, and ecclesiastical history (CIC 1385). The practice of censorship has been submitted to criticism quite often in recent times, and it is probable that the Roman Church will abandon this particular form of imperialism in learning.

Did this obviously hoped for change take place? Again we turn to *The New Code of Canon Law*:

> In order for the integrity of the truths of the faith and morals to be preserved, the pastors of the Church have the duty and the right to be vigilant lest harm be done to the faith or morals of the Christian faithful through writings or the use of the instruments of social communication; they likewise have the duty and the right to demand that writings to be published by the Christian faithful which touch upon faith or morals be submitted to their judgment; they also have the duty and right to denounce writings which harm correct faith or good morals (Canon 823, #1).

> Unless otherwise evident, the prescriptions of the canons of this title concerning books are to be applied to any writings whatsoever which are destined for public distribution (Canon 824, #2).

> Without a just and reasonable cause the Christian faithful are not to write anything for newspapers, magazines, or periodicals which are accustomed to attack openly the Catholic religion or good morals; clerics and members of religious institutes are to do so only with the permission of the local ordinary (Canon 831, #1).

Do not be deceived. The underlying beliefs of the Roman Catholic hierarchy, which was behind it all, have not really changed. It is the same old thing.

So *The New Code of Canon Law* arrived, and its arrival was trumpeted in the Catholic periodicals. The language was different; the number of canons had been drastically reduced. But was it new, different, and ecumenical? Do not be deceived. The underlying beliefs of the Roman Catholic hierarchy, which was behind it all, have not really changed. It is the same old thing.

Infant Baptism in the Roman Catholic Church

When I was a child, just a few weeks old, my parents took me to St. John's the Evangelist Church in Cincinnati, Ohio, to be baptized into the Roman Catholic Church. Over the years I witnessed many christenings and even served as a godparent in one of them, not questioning the necessity of what was being done. Roman Catholics are taught that it is their solemn responsibility to see to it that their children, as infants, are baptized. *The New Code of Canon Law* states, "Parents are obliged to see to it that infants are baptized within the first weeks after birth; as soon as possible after the birth or even before it, parents are to go to the pastor to request the sacrament for their child and to be properly prepared for it" (Canon 867).

"Catholic parents who put off for a long time, or entirely neglect, the Baptism of their children, commit a mortal sin."

The Baltimore Catechism that I studied as a student in parochial school was even clearer concerning the obligation upon parents to have their infants baptized when it said, "Catholic parents who put off for a long time, or entirely neglect, the Baptism of their children, commit a mortal sin." Roman Catholics are taught that infant baptism was a tradition begun with the Apostles and continued uninterrupted to the present time.

The Second Vatican Council restated the necessity of infant baptism. One of the *Post Conciliar Documents*, the "Instruction on Infant Baptism" from

October 20, 1980, prepared by the Sacred Congregation for the Doctrine of the Faith, stated, "Both in the East and in the West the practice of baptizing infants is considered a rule of *immemorial tradition*. Origen, and later Saint Augustine, considered it a 'tradition received from the Apostles.'"

In actuality, infant baptism is not a tradition "received from the Apostles." The earliest indication of it to be found is from A.D. 180, approximately 100 years after the death of the last apostle. Infant baptism was not continued uninterrupted through the centuries. Even in the Catholic Church, various popes and councils had to constantly reaffirm and defend the practice up to the Council of Trent. And still today the practice is not unquestioned, as we shall see from the *Post Conciliar Document*, "Instruction on Infant Baptism." Infant baptism is based on the traditions of men and not God. It cannot be found in the pages of God's Word, and Roman Catholic authorities will candidly admit that. We will see that it truly can be classified as a "tradition of men," about which Jesus said, "But in vain they do worship me, teaching for doctrines the commandments of men" (Matt. 15:9).

The Development of Infant Baptism

The "Instruction on Infant Baptism" states, "When the first direct evidence of infant baptism appears in the second century, it is never presented as an innovation. Saint Irenaeus, in particular, considers it a matter of course that the baptized should include 'infants and small children' as well as adolescents, young adults and older people."

The actual quote from Irenaeus' *Against Heresies* is, "For he came to save all by means of himself—all, I say, who by him are born again to God—infants, children, adolescents, young men, and old men" (II, xxii. 4). As you can see, there is no specific reference to baptism in this statement, although "born again" may refer to it. In Irenaeus' writings the word that generally refers to baptism for him is "regeneration," a different word from the one used here.

The first specific unambiguous reference to infant baptism is found in Tertullian's, *On Baptism*, and he was opposed to the practice. Tertullian wrote in the early third century.

Going back to "Instruction on Infant Baptism" we find, "The oldest known ritual, describing at the start of the third century the *Apostolic Tradition*, contains the following rule: 'First baptize the children. Those of them who can speak for themselves should do so. The parents or someone of their family should speak for the others.'"

When one quotes from a source, it is only fair that the quote be either given in context or explained contextually. The Sacred Congregation for the Doctrine of the Faith did not do so. From the book, *Early Christians Speak*, by Everett Ferguson, we have this explanation of the statements concerning baptism in *Apostolic Tradition*:

> Hippolytus in the *Apostolic Tradition* (v. 13) tells us how baptism was administered in the early third century, and presumably he is describing practices which in their main outlines if not in all details reach back into the second century. His baptismal ceremony is clearly designed for those of responsible age, who can pass through a catechumenate, fast, renounce the Devil, confess their faith, and join in the communion. This description, as all the other ancient liturgies of baptism, clearly presupposes those of accountable age, and the provision for sponsors was an awkward adjustment for those who could not answer for themselves. The confession of faith was considered so integral to the baptism act that it could not be dispensed with even for those unable to make their own confession (60).

Thus far we have seen that the earliest evidence of infant baptism was almost 100 years after the death of the last apostle, and it was hardly conclusive. The first unquestioned reference to infant baptism was from the third century and was opposed to it. The statement from *Apostolic Tradition* was wrenched from its context by the Sacred Congregation for the Doctrine of the Faith and did not so clearly support infant baptism as they would have us to believe.

Origen wrote in A.D. 225 and provides the first claim that infant baptism was an apostolic custom delivered to the church. It is important to note, however, as Everett Ferguson writes, "Of the passages from Origen on infant baptism only the one from *Homilies on Luke* (v. 14) survives in Greek, and his Latin translators were not always faithful. Origen did refer to infant baptism, but perhaps full confidence cannot be put in every phrase found only in the Latin."

As the fourth century came around, even the Sacred Congregation for the Doctrine of the Faith says, "Admittedly there was a certain decline in the practice of infant baptism during the fourth century." My friends, this now places us almost 300 years removed from the time of Christ and there is still no evidence of a generally believed, accepted and practiced rite of infant baptism. How can it possibly be said that it was "a rule of *immemorial tradition*"?

Allow me to quote, once again, from the *Post Conciliar Document,* "Instruction on Infant Baptism," to show that disagreement concerning infant baptism was the norm for the Catholic Church rather than the exception. It says:

> Later the Council of Carthage in 418 condemned "whoever says that newborn infants should not be baptized," and it taught that, on account of the church's "rule of faith" concerning original sin, "even babies, who are yet unable to commit any sin personally, are truly baptized for the forgiveness of sins, for the purpose of cleansing by rebirth what they have received by birth."

(*Historically, infant baptism, followed by infant sinfulness, followed by original sin was the progression of the theology—g.l.).

> This teaching was constantly reaffirmed and defended during the Middle Ages. In particular, the Council of Vienna in 1312 stressed that the sacrament of baptism has for its effect, in the case of infants, not just the forgiveness of sins but also the granting of grace and virtues. The Council of Florence in 1442 rebuked those who wanted baptism postponed and declared that infants should receive "as soon as convenient" the sacrament "through which they are rescued from the devil's power and adopted as God's children."

The Council of Trent repeated the Council of Carthage's condemnation, and referring to the words of Jesus to Nicodemus, it declared, "Since the promulgation of the Gospel" nobody can be justified "without being washed for rebirth or wishing to be." One of the errors anathematized by the Council is the Anabaptist view that "it is better that the baptism (of children) be omitted than to baptize in the faith of the Church alone those who do not believe by their own act."

This document goes on and mentions various regional councils and synods that upheld "with equal firmness" the teaching of the Council of Trent concerning baptizing children. The very fact that so many reaffirmations and so much defense of infant baptism were necessary proves that it was not a "rule of immemorial tradition" or a "tradition received from the Apostles."

Scriptural Proof?

If, in fact, infant baptism is a tradition received from the apostles, it would stand to reason that the apostles said something about it, and the practice could be found in the pages of the New Testament. Even the Sacred Congregation for the Doctrine of the Faith knows that infant baptism is not found in God's Word. In "Instruction on Infant Baptism" we find:

Noting that in the New Testament writings baptism follows the preaching of the Gospel, presupposes conversion and goes with a profession of faith, and furthermore that the effects of grace (forgiveness of sins, justification, rebirth and sharing in divine life) are generally linked with faith rather than with the sacrament, some people propose that the order "preaching, faith, sacrament" should become the rule. . . .It is *beyond doubt* that the preaching of the Apostles was normally directed to adults, and the first to be baptized were people converted to the Christian faith. *As these facts are related in the books of the New Testament,* they could give rise to the opinion that it is only the faith of adults that is considered in these texts. However, as was mentioned above, the practice of baptizing children rests on an *immemorial tradition originating from the Apostles* (107-108).

So you see, the Sacred Congregation for the Doctrine of the Faith admits that the apostles said nothing about infant baptism, nor did their practice as recorded in the pages of the New Testament include infant baptism.

So you see, the Sacred Congregation for the Doctrine of the Faith admits that the apostles said nothing about infant baptism, nor did their practice as recorded in the pages of the New Testament include infant baptism. But they brush those facts aside and say that infant baptism was an "immemorial tradition originating from the Apostles." Such reasoning not only fails to make sense, it is not true.

Infant baptism is a tradition of men, which Jesus said renders worship vain. As such, it must be rejected.

The Roman Catholic View of Birth Control

One of the more widely known beliefs of the Roman Catholic Church concerns the matter of birth control. A great many people are aware that the Roman Catholic hierarchy forbids the use of any "artificial" means that prevents conception. In Pope Paul VI's famous encyclical, *Humanae Vitae*, of July 25, 1968, he stated their position in the following manner:

> Therefore we base our words on the first principles of a human and Christian doctrine of marriage when we are obliged once more to declare that the direct interruption of the generative process already begun and, above all, direct abortion, even for therapeutic reasons, are to be absolutely excluded as lawful means of controlling the birth of children.

> Equally to be condemned, as the Magisterium of the Church has affirmed on various occasions, is direct sterilization, whether of the man or of the woman, whether permanent or temporary.

> Similarly excluded is any action, which either before, at the moment of, or after sexual intercourse, is specifically intended to prevent procreation—whether as an end or as a means.

> Neither is it valid to argue, as a justification for sexual intercourse which is deliberately contraceptive, that a lesser evil is to be preferred to a greater one, or that such intercourse would merge with the normal relations of past and future to form a single entity, and so be qualified by exactly the same moral goodness as these. Though it is true that sometimes it is lawful to tolerate a lesser moral evil in order to avoid a greater or in order to promote a greater good, it is never lawful, even for the gravest reasons, to do evil that good may come of it— in other words, to intend positively something which intrinsically contradicts

the moral order, and which must therefore be judged unworthy of man, even though the intention is to protect or promote the welfare of an individual, of a family or of society in general. Consequently it is a serious error to think that a whole married life of otherwise normal relations can justify sexual intercourse, which is deliberately contraceptive and so intrinsically wrong.

Most are also aware that the Roman Catholic Church does permit its members to use the "Rhythm Method" to attempt to regulate the births in their families. This was also set forth by Pope Paul VI in *Humanae Vitae* when he wrote:

> If therefore there are reasonable grounds for spacing births, arising from the physical or psychological condition of husband or wife, or from external circumstances, the Church teaches that then married people may take advantage of the natural cycles imminent in the reproductive system and use their marriage at precisely those times that are infertile, and in this way control birth, a way which does not in the least offend the moral principles which we have just explained.

This prohibition of artificial means of birth control is not a new idea of the Roman Catholic Church. We can find suggestions of it as early as the fourth century when Lactantius wrote, "Everyone should remember that the union of the two sexes is meant only for the purpose of procreation."

Augustine, in the fifth century, wrote, "Intercourse with even a lawful wife is unlawful and wicked if the conception of offspring is prevented."

In the seventeenth century, Francis De Sales stated:

> Nuptial commerce, which is so holy, just and commendable in itself, and so profitable to the commonwealth, is, nevertheless, in certain cases dangerous to those who exercise it, as when the order appointed for the procreation of children is violated and perverted; in which case, according as one departs more or less from it, the sins are more or less abominable, but always mortal.

So according to Roman Catholic teaching, the use of any method of birth control other than the rhythm method constitutes a mortal sin and will cause those so doing to perish in hell if they refuse to repent of those actions. The question that comes to mind, however, is how many Roman Catholics realize that even the use of the rhythm method is strictly regulated by the Catholic Church and that the morality of practicing it on a consistent basis is questioned?

Pope Pius XII, in a talk he gave to the Italian midwives on October 29, 1951 on the morality of the use of the rhythm method, made these statements:

If the carrying out of this theory means nothing more than a couple can make use of their matrimonial rights on the days of natural sterility too, there is nothing against it, for by so doing they neither hinder nor injure in any way the consummation of the natural act and its further natural consequences. . . . If, however, it is a further question—that is, of permitting the conjugal act on those days exclusively—then the conduct of the married couple must be examined more closely. Here two other hypotheses present themselves to us. If at the time of marriage at least one of the couple intended to restrict the marriage right, not merely its use, to the sterile periods, in such a way that at other times the second party would not even have the right to demand the act, this would imply an essential defect in the consent to marriage, which would carry with it invalidity of the marriage itself, because the right deriving from the contract of marriage is a permanent, uninterrupted and not intermittent right of each of the parties, one to the other.

On the other hand, if the act be limited to the sterile periods in so far as the mere use and not the right is concerned, there is no question about the validity of the marriage. Nevertheless, the moral licitness of such conduct on the part of the couple would have to be approved or denied, according as to whether or not the intention of observing those periods constantly was based on sufficient and secure moral grounds. The mere fact that the couple do not offend the nature of the act and are prepared to accept and bring up the child which in spite of their precautions came into the world would not be sufficient in itself to guarantee the rectitude of intention and the unobjectionable morality of the motives themselves.

So the Roman Catholic Church reaches into the bedroom of its followers and seeks to question the motives of its members who choose to use even the authorized method of birth control of that church. For those men who never know the responsibility of providing for and caring for children, such is easy. For those who do know the responsibility and face it daily, the right to regulate the number of births in their family is their own. God places the responsibility of providing for the physical needs of a family upon the shoulders of the father, with the wife acting as his partner in the enterprise. They know how many they can adequately provide for.

1 Corinthians 7:1-5 certainly indicates that procreation is not the sole purpose for sexual activity between husbands and wives. And Hebrews 13:4 tells us, "Marriage is honorable in all, and the bed undefiled." God has given these rights and responsibilities to the parents, not a group of unmarried men in Rome.

The Roman Catholic View
of Education

In the system of Roman Catholicism, a great deal of emphasis is placed upon the duty of parents to provide for the education of their children. This duty is stated in the 1917 *Code of Canon Law*: "Parents are bound by a most serious obligation to provide to the best of their ability for the religious and moral as well as the physical and civil education of their children, and also to provide for their temporal welfare" (Canon 1113). *The New Code of Canon Law* states this obligation: "Parents as well as those who take their place are obligated and enjoy the right to educate their offspring; Catholic parents also have the duty and the right to select those means and institutions through which they can provide more suitably for the Catholic education of their children according to local circumstances" (Canon 793, #1).

Most Roman Catholics take this obligation very seriously and because of it, particularly in the United States, two almost entirely separate and distinct school systems have arisen—the parochial and the public. As early as 1884 the American Catholic hierarchy, meeting at the Third Council of Baltimore, decreed, "Near each church, where it does not yet exist, a parochial school is to be erected within two years from the promulgation of this Council and is to be maintained in perpetuity, unless the bishop, on account of grave difficulties, judges that a postponement be allowed." By 1962 there were in the United States alone 10,760 parochial grade schools with an enrollment of approximately 4,700,000, and 2,432 high schools with an approximate enrollment of 900,000. At that time it meant that about one out of every seven children was enrolled in a Roman Catholic school.

In order to understand such a massive school system operated by this organization, one must understand the Roman Catholic view to education overall. In 1864 Pope Pius IX, in his famous *Syllabus of Errors* (a document that has never been renounced by the Roman Catholic Church) made the following statements in Propositions 45, 47, and 48:

> The direction of public schools in which the youth of Christian states are brought up . . . neither can nor ought to be assumed by the civil authority alone, or in such a manner that no right shall be recognized on the part of any other authority to interfere in the dispositions of the schools, in the regulation of the studies, in the appointment of degrees, and in the selection and approval of masters. . . .It is false that the best conditions of civil society demand that popular schools be open to the children of all classes, or that the generality of public institutions should be free from all ecclesiastical authority. Catholics cannot approve a system of education for youth apart from the Catholic faith, and disjointed from the authority of the church.

Statements such as this have been made because the Roman Catholic Church's hierarchy believes that they, and they alone, have the right to educate. By that, I mean to education, period. In 1929 Pope Pius IX, in his encyclical, *On the Education of Youth*, wrote, "In the first place, education belongs preeminently to the Church for two supernatural reasons. . . .As for the scope of the Church's educative mission, it extends over all people without limitations, according to Christ's command, 'Teach ye all nations.' Nor is there a power which can oppose or prevent it."

Even *The New Code of Canon Law* teaches the same idea in somewhat softer language, when it states, "The duty and right of educating belongs in a unique way to the Church which has been divinely entrusted with the mission to assist men and women so they can arrive at the fullness of the Christian life" (Canon 794, #1).

Now obviously in a democratic country such as the United States, such sentiments are not going to sit too well, so the Roman Catholic officials have devised this method to deal with it. In the *Pastoral Letter of the American Catholic Hierarchy*, 1919, they stated, "The State has a right to insist that its citizens shall be educated." This statement has given the Catholic hierarchy a means whereby they can shield from the general populace their true attitude concerning education. Let me give you an example. In *The Question Box* by Bertrand L. Conway, a Paulist priest, the following questions and answers appear:

Why are Catholics hostile to the public schools? Why do they have separate schools? Is this not un-American? Do Catholics recognize the State's right to educate its citizens? Has the parent or the State the primary duty in education?

Catholics are not hostile to the public schools; they are critical of them—a totally different position. They cannot on principle accept the present system of public education in the United States, because it does not give Catholic children the moral and religious training which they consider essential. As citizens who pay their proportionate share of the State's school tax, they have a right to criticize a defective State system of education.

The State has a right to insist upon its citizens being educated, but it has no right to hamper private initiative, or to establish a State monopoly on education (213-214).

That all sounds good. Yes, the state has the right to insist upon its citizens being educated, but according to Pope Pius XI, even those public schools would have to be overseen by the Roman Catholic Church. He said, "As for the scope of the Church's educative mission, it extends over all people without any limitations." *The Question Box* is a book written specifically for non-Catholic readers. What position is taken in a book which would not have such wide distribution? Rev. J. A. Burns, president of Holy Cross College in Washington, D.C., wrote in his book, *The Growth and Development of the Catholic School System in the United States,* "We deny, of course, as Catholics, the right of the civil government to educate, for education is a function of the spiritual society. . . .It (the state) may found and endow schools and pay the teachers, but it cannot dictate or interfere with the education or discipline of the schools" (223).

> **Yes, the state has the right to insist upon its citizens being educated, but according to Pope Pius XI, even those public schools would have to be overseen by the Roman Catholic Church.**

Perhaps the majority of the Roman Catholic laity is not hostile to public schools, but what about the hierarchy? Paul L. Blakely, S.J., in an article entitled, *May An American Oppose the Public School?* (which, by the way, bears the Imprimatur of the late Cardinal Hayes), as quoted by Loraine Boettner in *Roman Catholicism* wrote:

Our first duty to the public schools is not to pay taxes for its maintenance. We pay that tax under protest, not because we admit an obligation in justice. . . .The first duty of every Catholic father to the public school is to keep his children out of it. . . .For the man who sends his children to the public school when he could obtain for them the blessing of a Catholic education is not a practicing Catholic, even though he goes to Mass every morning!

The 1917 *Code of Canon Law* stated:

Catholic children should not attend non-Catholic, neutral, or mixed schools, that is, those which are open also to non-Catholics. It pertains exclusively to the ordinary of the place to decide in accordance with instructions of the Holy See, under what circumstances and with what safeguards against the danger of perversion of the faith attendance at such schools may be tolerated (Canon 1374).

Such statements certainly indicate hostility to the average reader. It is important to note that in communities where it is possible, Catholics are required to send their children to a parochial school. *The New Code of Canon Law* states, "Parents are to entrust their children to those schools in which Catholic education is provided; but if they are unable to do this, they are bound to provide for their suitable Catholic education outside the schools" (Canon 798).

So the two school systems exist in the United States. In recent years, however, declining enrollment and the profound drop in the number of nuns available has created difficulty for the Catholic Church as far as maintaining its system is concerned. In Cincinnati, Ohio, several schools have closed, numerous high schools have merged, and the elementary school that I attended as a child, which had an enrollment of almost 900 when I was there, is down to about 350 students. It is becoming financially more difficult for the Roman Catholic hierarchy to keep their system open, as it has existed. One thing is certain, however. Even in the face of these difficulties, even as the hierarchy makes concessions due to financial considerations, their beliefs concerning education have not changed, nor will they.

Which Roman Catholic Church? Vatican II

As a youngster growing up within the confines of Roman Catholicism, I spent every weekday morning attending 8:00 Mass at St. John's the Evangelist in Cincinnati, Ohio. The nuns, who were our teachers, would lead each class into the church building to sit in our assigned seats and watch the sacrament of Holy Eucharist take place. The language of the Mass was Latin, which none of us understood. We did not understand the significance of each part of the Mass, nor the symbolism involved, but we knew by heart our assigned responses and would join in wholeheartedly at the appropriate times. If the day happened to be the first Friday of the month, we would receive a special treat. All of us would receive Communion on that day, and since it was necessary to fast from midnight until Communion had been received, the cafeteria would be opened after Mass for breakfast. We did not fully understand the necessity of the fast; we simply knew that it was a sin not to do so.

Sunday was a particularly special day, for on that day my entire family would attend 11:00 Mass to fulfill the requirement of worshipping God on Sunday by assisting at the holy sacrifice of the Mass. It was exciting to see the large number of my fellow Catholics gathered together doing the things that I had been taught all Christians had done since the time of Christ. We were a peculiar people, different from all the others, and the only ones destined to go to heaven; for there was no salvation outside the one true church, the Holy Roman Catholic Church. Together we were following Jesus more closely than others. We were the only ones who did not eat meat on Fridays, for to do so was a sin. We were the ones who had an unmarried clergy, just like Jesus was unmarried. We were the ones who were led by the infallible Pope, the Vicar of Christ and successor to Saint Peter. I was taught, as were all Catholics, that these things we did and believed had always been done and believed by all Christians from the time that Jesus established the church until now. There was comfort in this knowledge. Even though we did not understand many of the things the Church required, we were secure in the belief that this was the way it had always been, and that it was the way it would always be. The Roman Catholic Church was truth, and truth did not change. Catholics found solace and comfort in that belief.

Then came the years of 1962-1965 and an event that radically changed the face of Roman Catholicism as it then existed. On October 11, 1962, 2,540 bishops and others of the Roman Catholic Church gathered in Rome for the opening solemn session of Vatican II. By the time of the final solemn session, held December 8, 1965, the comfort and solace that so many Roman Catholics had found in their Church had been shattered. For many Roman Catholics, there was confusion. For many elderly Roman Catholics there was a feeling of betrayal. How could the things that they had been taught and practiced for so many years no longer be true or required? And for many younger Catholics, there had been enough. The Roman Catholic Church, the Church of the Fathers, had changed many of its practices, its beliefs, and quite obviously, its direction.

In the remainder of this chapter, we are going to notice several of the changes. Many of them were quite obvious and real; others were changes in word only. An important question to consider is, "Which Roman Catholic Church?" Was the one prior to Vatican II, led by an infallible Pope and teaching Magisterium, right? Or is the one in existence now, also led by an infallible Pope and teaching Magisterium, right? They both cannot be right, for they are most definitely different. Or does the question itself prove that neither one was the true Church of Christ?

The Language of the Mass

One of the most obvious changes to occur within Roman Catholicism since Vatican II involves the language used in the Mass. Prior to the Council, the Mass was said in Latin. Most Roman Catholics would be surprised to learn that the original language was Greek and that Latin did not supercede it until the early fifth century. Actually, the earliest extant liturgy of the Roman Church Latin worship dates from the sixth century. Nonetheless, from the fifth century on, the language was Latin.

Vatican II instituted changes in this area. From *The Constitution of the Sacred Liturgy* we find: "(1) The use of the Latin language, with due respect to particular law, is to be preserved in the Latin rites. (2) But since the use of the vernacular, whether in the Mass, the administration of the sacraments, or in other parts of the liturgy, may frequently be of great advantage to the people, a wider use may be made of it, especially in readings, directives, and in some prayers and chants" (Section C, #36).

With the directive of Vatican II, the Mass could now be said in the common language of the people involved. This change did not come without dissent. Even today, over forty years after the Council, most major metropolitan areas still have one or two Catholic Churches that have refused to accept the common vernacular and cling to the old Latin way. Most of these churches are attended by elderly Roman Catholics.

Fasting

Another change that has taken place and can be associated with the direction of Vatican II involves the time of fasting required of a Roman Catholic before he or she can receive Holy Communion. As a child, pre-Vatican II, I was taught from *The Baltimore Catechism* that to receive Holy Communion, one was required to fast from midnight to the time of reception. The fast was defined in this way: "To fast from midnight means to take nothing by way of food or drink or medicine after midnight." The seriousness of this requirement can be seen in the book, *The Eucharist (Law and Practice)* by P. Durieux. He wrote:

> It (fast before communion) consists in this, that the communicant has not taken, since midnight, after food or drink or medicine, even the least possible quantity. It would be a mortal sin to receive Communion after having intentionally taken a few drops of water after midnight, even an error of good faith (e.g., the taking of a drink of water at two o'clock in the morning because the clock had stopped at a quarter before twelve), does not dispense from the law.

The only time a person could receive Holy Communion without the midnight fast was if they were in danger of dying or if the Eucharist itself was in danger of injury or insult. Failure to abide by this fast was a mortal sin according to the infallible teaching of the Roman Catholic Church.

During and since Vatican II changes have come concerning this fast. The time for the fast went first from midnight to three hours. Then in 1964 it went from three hours to one hour at the decree of Pope Paul VI. The latest regulation is found in *The New Code of Canon Law*, from 1983: "One who is to receive the Most Holy Eucharist is to abstain from any food or drink with the exception only of water and medicine, for at least the period of one hour before Holy Communion" (Canon 919).

Such a change forced many Catholics to question their Church. How can that which was a mortal sin cease to be a mortal sin simply because a group of men say so? Furthermore, what of those who had died with the mortal sin of not fasting from midnight before receiving Holy Communion still held against them? Are they to perish in hell for something that is no longer even a sin? Which Church was right—the Catholic Church prior to Vatican II or the one after Vatican II?

Meat on Fridays

Another change ushered in by the direction taken in Vatican II involves the eating of meat on Friday, at least in America. In the years before Vatican II Catholics were taught that Friday was a day of abstinence. A day of abstinence was a day on which no meat was permitted to be eaten. Of Friday, *The Baltimore Catechism* said, "The Church makes Fridays a day of abstinence to remind us of Our Lord's death on Good Friday." This was one of the chief six laws of the church according to #281 in *The Baltimore Catechism*. To violate it was to sin. Now Catholics can eat meat on Fridays in the United States. Which was right—to eat meat on Fridays or not to eat meat on Fridays? If it was a sin before, why isn't it a sin now?

Most Roman Catholics in America would be surprised to learn that in other countries the abstinence from meat on Fridays is still required, and it is a part of the 1983 *New Code of Canon Law*, Canons 1251 and 1252.

Sunday Attendance at Mass

Still another obvious change that can be traced to the direction taken by Vatican II has to do with Sunday attendance at Mass. Quite simply, prior to Vatican II Catholics were required, under pain of mortal sin, to attend Mass on Sundays. Again from *The Baltimore Catechism* we find, "A Catholic who through his own fault misses Mass on a Sunday or holy day of obligation commits a mortal sin" (#282).

Today Roman Catholic churches throughout the United States have Saturday evening Masses that can act as substitutes for Sunday attendance. If a Catholic attends a Saturday evening Mass, he or she is not obligated to go on Sunday as well. Such a thing was unheard of prior to Vatican II. I distinctly remember the first time I heard of this new regulation. I was still a young boy and attended a wedding on a Saturday evening at my parish church. I had attended numerous Saturday evening weddings before, but what made this one different was that after the ceremony, which was a Nuptial Mass, the priest told us that our attendance there took care of our Sunday obligation. As a young boy, I was tickled because that meant I would not have to go to services the next day. Years later, in light of previously received teaching, I wondered how such a change could be made.

The Shortage of Religious Vocations

Another change that should be mentioned has to do with the declining number of priests and nuns. As a boy in parochial school, I was taught almost exclusively by nuns. There are no longer any nuns at the school I attended. In Cincinnati there were two seminaries—a major seminary and a minor seminary. Now there is only one. Throughout the world, Roman Catholicism is suffering from a rapid decline in what they call religious vocations. The shortage of priests has reached epidemic proportions. Numerous Catholic educational facilities have closed because there are no nuns to teach in them, and hiring lay people is too expensive.

It is my personal belief that one of the major causes of this situation was Vatican II. Roman Catholics of my age, those who would now be the priests and nuns, came to realize that that which could be changed so drastically and easily was not God's eternal truth. They came to realize that that which was sin yesterday had to be sin tomorrow, or you couldn't count on that which was truth yesterday still being truth tomorrow. Additionally, several priests and nuns who were personal friends during the time of Vatican II have since left their vocations. It is sometimes difficult for one who was not a Catholic during those tumultuous years to fully understand how drastically the Roman Catholic Church was changed.

Confession and Absolution

There have been other, less obvious changes in the practices of the Roman Catholic Church since Vatican II. For instance, changes have occurred in the sacrament of Penance, most commonly know as "going to confession." Prior to Vatican II, this was done by the penitent entering into a confessional and telling his or her sins to the priest. This is made quite clear in *The Baltimore Catechism* where we find," Confession is the telling of our sins to an authorized priest for the purpose of obtaining forgiveness" (315). When this was done the priest would give a penance, generally the saying of a certain number of prayers, and then grant absolution. Since the *Post Conciliar Document of Vatican II*, entitled "Introduction to the New Order of Penance," there has been a wider use of what is called "general absolution." The document states:

> Individual and integral confession and absolution remains the only ordinary way by which the faithful may be reconciled with God and with the Church, except when this is physically or morally impossible. It can happen that, because of a particular combination of circumstances, absolution may be, or even ought to be, given to a number of people together, without individual confession of sins.

More and more this "general absolution" is being granted in the course of the Mass. Is this due to a lack of priests? I don't know for certain, but it certainly was not practiced, or allowed, prior to Vatican II.

Celibacy of the Priests

Another change, much less obvious and rarely spoken of, concerns the celibacy of the priests. From the *Post Conciliar Document*, "Encyclical Letter on Priestly Celibacy," by Pope Paul VI we read:

> In virtue of the fundamental norm of the government of the Catholic Church, to which we alluded above, while, on the one hand, the law requiring a freely chosen and perpetual celibacy of those who are admitted to Holy Orders remains unchanged, on the other hand, a study may be allowed of the particular circumstances of married sacred ministers of Churches or other Christian communities separated from the Catholic communion, and of the possibility of admitting to priestly functions those who desire to adhere to the fullness of this communion and to continue to exercise the sacred ministry. The circumstances must be such, however, as not to prejudice the existing discipline regarding celibacy (#42).

Recently, married Episcopal priests have been permitted to become Roman Catholic priests while remaining married. They merely pledge adherence to Roman Catholicism, particularly allegiance to the Pope. Many Catholics have wondered why celibacy continues to be required of some if it can be set aside for others.

Ecumenicalism

Many also have wondered about the ecumenical sounds that have been coming from Roman Catholicism since the time of Vatican II. One of the largest documents to come out of the Council was the *Decree on Ecumenism* on November 21, 1964. Pre-Vatican II teaching on this subject was very clear. *The Baltimore Catechism* said, "All are obliged to belong to the Catholic

Church in order to be saved" (129). This same doctrine was often expressed as, "Outside the Church there is no salvation." The only ones outside of the Catholic Church who could be saved were those who, through no fault of their own, were ignorant of the Church.

Since Vatican II we have seen Catholic priests taking part in ecumenical services and functions in various cities and at various times. Some have interpreted this as a move toward real ecumenicalism. Do not be deceived. The practices in this area have changed, but the underlying principles have not. We find this statement in the *Decree on Ecumenism:*

> This sacred Council firmly hopes that the initiatives of the sons of the Catholic Church, joined with those of the separated brethren, will go forward, without obstructing the ways of divine Providence, and without prejudging the future inspirations of the Holy Spirit. Further, this Council declares that it realizes that this holy objective—the reconciliation of all Christians in the unity of the one and only Church of Christ—transcends human powers and gifts.

The goal of Roman Catholic ecumenism is now, and always has been, the existence of only one church—the Roman Catholic Church.

What To Do?

What then is a Roman Catholic to do? Their church has changed. In many ways it is not the same church it was prior to Vatican II, and the changes will continue. Vatican II set the Catholic Church on the path to change. What was true yesterday may not necessarily be true tomorrow.

For the one who would be a true follower of Jesus Christ and who seeks to do His will, there is only one answer. Paul gave it when he wrote, "Wherefore come out from among them, and be ye separate, saith the Lord, and touch not the unclean thing; and I will receive you, and will be a Father unto you, and ye shall be my sons and daughters, saith the Lord Almighty" (2 Cor. 6:17-18).

So What Do We Do Now?

In the course of this book we have examined practically all of the major doctrines peculiar to Roman Catholicism. We have studied what that Church teaches, the historical development of each doctrine, and where and when they deviated from the truth of God's revealed Word. As my labor in this work draws to a close, one thing breaks my heart and, if I allow it to, brings tears to my eyes. While difficult to articulate, that one thing is the fact that the vast majority of Catholics, particularly in the United States of America, know very little about the history of what their Church teaches. They know very little about the development of the doctrines that they are bound to uphold. They know very little about the true attitude of their hierarchy toward those who are not Catholic, and most have heard nothing, or very little, about the blackest spot in their history, the Inquisition. I wish I could do more.

It should be stated that there is much in the Roman Catholic Church that is true. Some of their doctrines contain much that is revealed in the Scriptures. As I was writing this book, I could not help but think of my years as a Roman Catholic and what my response would have been in those days to many of the statements I had written. It would not have been very favorable. Yet, with little knowledge of what my Church actually taught, and even less knowledge of the Bible, how was I to know?

I know that most Roman Catholics have no idea that papal infallibility was not declared to be a doctrine of the Church until 1870. Most Roman Catholics have no idea that it was not until November 1, 1950 that the bodily assumption of Mary into heaven was declared to be a dogma of their Church. I know these things because I was there.

For those who are familiar with the Bible this may be hard to believe, but as a Roman Catholic I had no idea that the Bible calls all Christians saints and that the whole Roman Catholic system of canonization is just something that developed over the years at the urging of the Catholic hierarchy. I was taught to pray to the saints and had no idea that even modern Roman Catholic authorities must, and do, admit that their Church canonized some people who never actually existed.

As a child in parochial schools, I went to May Festivals. These were ceremonies meant to honor Mary. I prayed to Mary, knelt before statutes of Mary, said the rosary, and believed that Mary was an intercessor for me to God. I was thoroughly indoctrinated with this belief and was never once taught that the first century church knew nothing about this adoration, or hyperdulia, that is given to Mary. I had no idea that the last time we read of Mary in the New Testament is in Acts 1:14. I had no idea that much of what the Roman Catholic Church teaches concerning Mary comes from different legends and apocryphal works that can in no way be substantiated and, in fact, show themselves to be questionable at best and downright untrue at worst. I didn't know all of this because I was never taught it.

As a young Catholic growing up I knew that the priests did not marry, I knew that they were celibate; but I honestly believed that was the way it had always been because that is what I was taught. I did not know that celibacy was not a divine decree, that it was not a scriptural command, and that it was not according to the example of the apostles and other first century Christians. I didn't know that the demand for celibacy among Roman Catholic priests was nothing more than a "church" regulation that had evolved over the centuries, often in the face of severe opposition. I didn't know that this arbitrary "rule" had caused untold problems for the men involved, and for the Roman Catholic Church itself. I didn't know these things because I was never taught them.

So what is a Catholic, or anyone else, supposed to do? Heed the words of the Apostle Paul to Timothy found in 2 Timothy 2:15, "Study to show thyself approved unto God, a workman that needeth not to be ashamed, rightly dividing the word of truth." Don't allow anyone to tell you that you cannot understand God's Word without being told by a member of the clergy what it means. That is not what Paul wrote to the Ephesians in Ephesians 3:4: "Whereby, when ye read, ye may understand my knowledge in the mystery of Christ." Understand that God has revealed His will for man in the Scriptures, and that "all scripture is given by inspiration of God, and is profitable for doctrine, for reproof, for correction, for instruction in righteousness: that the man of God may be perfect, thoroughly furnished unto all good works" (2 Tim. 3:16-17).

As I sit back and read the quotation from 2 Timothy that I just referenced, I can hear the voices of Roman Catholic apologists crying out, "That is that old Protestant idea of *Sola Scriptura* (or 'the Bible only')." In the first place, I am not a Protestant; and in the second place, my friends, it is the simple truth. We have been given all things that pertain to life and godliness in the truth that was once delivered to the saints (2 Pet. 1:3; Jude 3). All must set aside their pride and previously held ideas, and submit in humble obedience to the will of Christ. Stand firmly on what the Bible actually says, and where God has been silent, respect His silence.

Truth does not fear investigation; it welcomes it. So, ask your priest about the things contained in this book. Refuse to take "no" for an answer and require that all answers have book, chapter, and verse from God's Word to substantiate them. If you find that the things you have been taught and have believed are simply not so, then follow Paul's advice found in 2 Corinthians 6:17-18, "Wherefore come out from among them, and be ye separate, saith the Lord, and touch not the unclean thing; and I will receive you, and will be a Father unto you, and ye shall be my sons and daughters, saith the Lord Almighty."

Bibliography

Alexander, Anthony. *College Moral Theology*. Chicago: Henry Regnery Co., 1957.

Baltimore Plenary Council. *A Catechism of Christian Doctrine*, Revised Edition, Baltimore Catechism, #3. Cincinnati: Christian Investigation Center Press, 1949.

Blanshard, Paul. *American Freedom and Catholic Power*. Boston: The Beacon Press, 1958.

Boettner, Loraine. *Roman Catholicism*. Phillipsburg: Presbyterian and Reformed Publishing Co., 1962.

Brunner, Emil. *Christianity and Civilization*. New York: C. Scribner's Sons, 1949.

Burns, J.A. *The Growth and Development of the Catholic School System in the United States*. New York: Benziger Bros., 1912.

Campbell, Alexander. *Debate on the Roman Catholic Religion*. Nashville: McQuiddy Printing Co., 1837.

Catholic Encyclopedia, ed. Knights of Columbus. New York: The Encyclopedia Press, 1913.

Catholic Reference Encyclopedia.. Minneapolis: Catholic Education Guild, 1968.

Cavanagh, John R., M.C. *Fundamental Marriage Counseling*. Milwaukee: The Bruce Publishing Co., 1958.

Chapin, John, ed., *The Book of Catholic Quotations*. New York: Farrar, Strauss, and Cudahy, 1956.

Colledge, Edmund. *The Catholic Layman's Library*. Gastonia: Good Will Publishers, Inc., 1970.

Connell, Father Francis J. *New Baltimore Catechism #3,* Confraternity Edition. Cincinnati: Benziger Brothers, Inc., 1949.

Conway, Bertrand L. *The Question Box*. New York: The Columbus Press, 1913.

_____. *The Question Box,* New Edition. New York: Paulist Press, 1929.

Conway, J. D., Monsignor. *What the Church Teaches*. New York: Harper & Brothers Publications, 1962

De Montford, St. Louis Mary. *True Devotion to the Blessed Virgin Mary*. New York: The Montford Fathers Publications, 1949.

Denzinger, Henry. *The Sources of Catholic Dogma*. Fitzwilliam: Loreto Publications, 1954.

Documents of Vatican II, New Revised Edition. Grand Rapids: William B.Eerdmans Publishing Co., 1984.

Donovan, C.F. *Our Faith and the Facts*. Chicago: Patrick L. Baine Publisher, 1929.

Durant, Will. *The Age of Faith*. New York: Simon and Schuster, 1950.

Durieux, P. *The Eucharist. Law and Practice*. Faribault, 1926.

Encyclopedia Americana. Danbury: Grolier, Inc., 1962.

Ferguson, Everett. *Early Christians Speak*. Austin: Sweet Publishing Co., 1971.

Flannery, Austin. *Vatican II, More Post Conciliar Documents*. Grand Rapids: Wm. B. Eerdmans Publishing Co., 1982

Gibbons, James Cardinal. *The Faith of Our Fathers*. Baltimore: Jno. Murphy Co., 1917.

Goldstein, David. *Campaigners for Christ Handbook*. Boston: T.J. Flynn & Co., Inc., 1934.

Grisar, Hartmann. *Martin Luther, His Life and Work*. Westminster: The Newman Press, 1961.

Hardon, Father John A., S.J. Archives, "Mariology" in *Collier's Encyclopedia*, Inter Mirifaca, 1998, *http://www.therealpresecne.org/archives/Mariology/Mariology/_025.htm*; Internet; accessed 16 December 2008.

Harris, R. Laird. *Fundamental Protestant Doctrines II*. booklet

Hefele, C. J. *History of the Christian Councils*. Edinburgh: T & T Clark, 1894.

Hill, Rev. John J. and Theodore C. Stone, Rev. *A Modern Catechism*. Chicago: Acta Foundation, 1964.

Keating, Karl. *Catholicism and Fundamentalism*. San Francisco: Ignatius Press, 1988.

Keenan, Stephen. *A Doctrinal Catechism*. New York: P.J. Kenedy and Sons, 1876.

Lauriere, M. Herve. *Assassins in the Name of God*. Paris: La Vigie, 1951.

Laux, John. *A Course in Religion for Catholic High Schools and Academies*. 1936.

Lea, Henry Charles. *History of Sacerdotal Celibacy in the Christian Church*. New York: Russell and Russell Publishing Co., 1957.

Lehmann, L. H. *The Soul of a Priest: My Conversion to the Pauline Succession*. New York: Agora Publications, 1933.

Liguori, Alphonse. *The Glories of Mary*, ed. Rev. Eugene Grimm. New York: Redemptorist Fathers, 1931, available from *http://www.marys-touch.com/Glories/contents.htm*; Internet; accessed 16 December 2008.

MacGregor, Geddes. *The Vatican Revolution*. Boston: MacMillan, 1958.

Martin, Malachi. *The Decline and Fall of the Roman Church*. New York: G.P. Putnam's Sons, 1983.

Martos, Joseph. *Doors to the Sacred*. Liguori: Liguori Publications, 1991.

Martyr, Justin. *Apology*. Grand Rapids: Wm. B. Eerdsman Publishing Co., 1989.

McKenzie, John L., S.J. *The Roman Catholic Church*. Austin: Holt, Rinehart, and Winston, 1969.

McLoughlin, Emmett. *American Culture & Catholic Schools*. New York: Lyle Stuart, Inc., 1960.

_____. *People's Padre: An Autobiography*. Boston: Beacon Press, 1954.

Newman, John Henry. *Loss and Gain: The Story of a Convert*. New York: Longman's Green and Co., 1906.

O'Brien, John A. *The Faith of Millions*. Huntington: Our Sunday Visitor, 1938.

O'Brien, John A. and others, eds. *Twenty-Five Questions Non-Catholics Ask*. Huntington: Our Sunday Visitor Press, 1958.

Orchard, Bernard. *A Catholic Commentary on Holy Scripture*. Nashville: Nelson Publishing Co., 1953.

Orr, James and others, eds. *The International Standard Bible Encyclopedia*. Grand Rapids: Wm. B. Eerdman Publishing Co., 1939.

Paris, Edmond. *Genocide in Satellite Croatia*. Chicago: The American Institute for Balkan Affairs, 1959.

_____. *The Vatican Against Europe*. London: Wickliffe Press, 1959.

Pastor, Ludwig. *History of the Popes*. 1928.

Pulpit Commentary on Catholic Teaching.. New York: Joseph F. Wagner, 1908.

Rose, Michael S. *Goodbye, Good Men*. Cincinnati: Aquinas Publishing Limited, 2002.

Ryan, John A. and Boland, Francis J. *Catholic Principles of Politics*. New York: McMillan Publishing Co., 1940.

Scheeben, Matthias Joseph and others, eds. *Manual of Catholic Theology*. London: K, Paul, Trench, Trubner, 1909.

Searle, George M. *Plain Facts for Fair Minds*. New York: Paulist Press, 1915.

Schadler, F. J. *The Beauties of the Catholic Church*, 26th Edition. New York: Frederick Postet & Co., 1881.

Tanis, Edward J. *What Rome Teaches*. South Holland: Progressive Calvinism League, 1954.

Tenney, Merrill C. *Zondervan Pictorial Encyclopedia of the Bible*. Grand Rapids: Zondervan, 1988.

Thayer, Joseph. *Thayer's Greek-English Lexicon of the New Testament.* Grand Rapids: Hendrickson Publishers, 1977.

The Catechism of the Catholic Church. Liguori: Liguori Publications, 1994.

The Catholic Encyclopedia Dictionary, John J. Wynne, et al, eds.. New York: The Gilmary Society, 1941.

The New Catholic Encyclopedia. ed. Catholic University of America. New York: McGraw-Hill Publications, 1967.

The New Code of Canon Law, Latin-English Edition. Washington, D.C.: Canon Law Society of America, 1983.

The New Merriam-Webster Pocket Dictionary. New York: Pocket Books, 1964.

Third Plenary Council of Baltimore. *The Baltimore Catechism,* Revised 1941 Edition, *http://www.catholicity.com/baltimore-catechism/lesson34.htm,* Internet; accessed 16 December 2008.

Vine, W. E. *Expository Dictionary of New Testament Words.* Old Tappan: Fleming H. Revell Co., 1966.

Walsh, Michael. *An Illustrated History of the Popes.* New York: St. Martin's Press, 1980.

Zacchello, Joseph. *Ins and Outs of Romanism.* New York: Loizeaux Brothers, 1956.

www.ingramcontent.com/pod-product-compliance
Lightning Source LLC
Chambersburg PA
CBHW072346090426
42741CB00012B/2935